200 bread recipes

D0529893

hamlyn | **all colour cookbook**

200 bread recipes

Joanna Farrow

An Hachette UK Company
www.hachette.co.uk

First published in Great Britain in 2009 by Hamlyn,
a division of Octopus Publishing Group Ltd,
2–4 Heron Quays, London E14 4JP
www.octopusbooks.co.uk

ISBN: 978-0-600-61933-8

A CIP catalogue record for this book is available from the
British Library

Printed and bound in China

1 2 3 4 5 6 7 8 9 10

Both metric and imperial measurements are given for the
recipes. Use one set of measures only, not a mixture of both.

Standard level spoon measures are used in all recipes:
1 tablespoon = one 15 ml spoon
1 teaspoon = one 5 ml spoon

Ovens should be preheated to the specified temperature.
If using a fan-assisted oven, follow the manufacturer's
instructions for adjusting the time and temperature.

Eggs should be medium unless otherwise stated; choose
free-range if possible and preferably organic. The Department
of Health advises that eggs should not be consumed raw.
This book contains some dishes made with raw or lightly
cooked eggs. It is prudent for more vulnerable people, such
as pregnant and nursing mothers, invalids, the elderly, babies
and young children, to avoid uncooked or lightly cooked
dishes made with eggs.

This book includes dishes made with nuts and nut
derivatives. It is advisable for those with known allergic
reactions to nuts and nut derivatives and those who may be
potentially vulnerable to these allergies, such as pregnant and
nursing mothers, invalids, the elderly, babies and children, to
avoid dishes made with nuts and nut oils. It is also prudent to
check the labels of preprepared ingredients for the possible
inclusion of nut derivatives.

The publisher is very grateful to Kenwood, Morphy
Richards and Panasonic for providing the bread machines
with which the recipes in this book were tested: Kenwood
BM250 Rapid Bake Breadmaker; Morphy Richards Accents
Breadmaker; Panasonic SD 255WXC Breadmaker.

contents

Introduction   6

basic breads   16

savoury breads   48

flat breads   90

individual breads   112

party breads   144

sweet breads   158

cakes   200

gluten-free breads   216

index   236

acknowledgements   240

introduction

Introduction

Bread-making machines are now one of the most popular and best loved 'kitchen gadgets', producing freshly baked bread at the flick of a switch and with minimal effort on behalf of the baker. For purists, the process of mixing, kneading and baking by hand is something that cannot be mimicked by a machine, but for most busy cooks a bread-making machine is a dream come true. What could be better than being able to programme freshly baked bread, ready and waiting for you either at breakfast time or later in the day for snacks or sandwiches or to accompany a main meal?

This book contains a comprehensive assortment of recipes, from basic loaves to enriched sweet and savoury breads, as well as gluten-free breads and recipes for teabreads and cakes. There are also plenty

of ideas for machine-made doughs, which are then layered, filled, shaped and baked conventionally, further extending the delicious range of fabulous breads that can be made with the machine.

ingredients

Most of the ingredients used in bread-machine baking are the same as those needed for making bread by hand, although for some, such as yeast, you will need to choose one specifically intended for bread-making machines.

yeast

Choose yeast that is labelled 'fast action' or 'easy blend'. This yeast, available in 7 g (about ¼ oz) sachets or small packs, is designed for mixing directly with the other bread ingredients. (Fresh and dried yeasts have to be fermented with liquids before they are added to the other ingredients.) It is important that you use precisely the amount of yeast specified in the recipes: too little will prevent the dough from rising and too much will make it collapse during baking. Store yeast in a cool, dry place where it will keep for several months.

flours

For a well-risen bread with a light, airy texture use 'strong bread flour', which is made from hard wheat and has a high gluten content. Strong brown or wholemeal flour contains bran and wheatgerm, making a well-flavoured bread with a nuttier, more fibrous texture. Because bran inhibits the action of the gluten, brown breads rise more slowly, and so the wholemeal or wholewheat programme on bread machines will be longer. Other wheat flours include malthouse and granary, which contain a mixture of white and wholemeal flours with added wheat grains, and these produce a well-flavoured loaf with a slightly nutty flavour and a rustic texture. Spelt flour is an ancient form of wheat flour. Lower in gluten, it produces a closer textured bread but with a good flavour, and it can be used in most of the recipes that use white flour. Non-wheat flours, including barley and rye, have low gluten contents and, used on their own, produce a heavier textured bread. For lighter results, mix these flours with strong white bread flour.

gluten-free flours

Gluten-free flours are ideal for anyone who has an intolerance to gluten. Available from supermarkets and health food stores, they usually contain a mixture of different flours, such as potato, rice and soya, in varying proportions. Some are specifically designed for use in bread-making machines and contain added natural gum, which helps imitate a more bread-like texture. Don't, however, expect gluten-free breads to taste like ordinary breads.

sugar

Sugar, which helps activate yeast, can be used in various forms, from caster to muscovado, maple syrup, honey or malt extract. If a large quantity of sugar is used, such as in teatime bread, the 'sweet' programme can be used so that the machine bakes at a lower temperature and stops the bread scorching around the edges. Do not use sugar substitutes.

salt

Salt is an essential ingredient in bread because it controls the rate at which the yeast ferments. If you don't like a salty flavour, use as little as half a teaspoon.

liquids

Unless you are using a fast/rapid bake programme, liquids are always added cold to the bread pan. Water and milk are the most frequently used, but other liquids, such as fruit juices, cider and yogurt, are sometimes added

for extra flavour. Don't use fresh milk if you are using the timer delay programme on your machine as the milk is likely to sour. Use water instead and add a couple of tablespoons of milk powder with the flour, if liked.

enriching ingredients

Butter, oil, eggs, cream and cheeses can be added to enrich doughs. Butter and oil also act as preservatives, keeping the bread fresher for longer. Use butter that's very soft rather than straight from the fridge, if necessary softening it in the microwave first. Do not use the timer delay programme if you are using dairy produce or other perishable ingredients.

herbs, spices and other flavouring

Chopped fresh or dried herbs, crushed or ground spices and other flavourings, such as vanilla, saffron and spicy pastes, can be used

to enhance the flavour of the most basic bread. Add the flavouring at the beginning of the programme with the flour if dry or the liquids if wet.

machine programmes

Selecting the right programme is essential for good results. Bread-making machines vary in the choice of programmes they offer, but those used in this book are the most often seen.

basic

This programme is probably the most useful and the one you'll keep returning to. It's used for basic white breads or breads in which white flour is the main ingredient. Enriched sweet and savoury breads can also be made using this programme.

wholewheat/wholemeal

Breads made using wholewheat or wholemeal flours have a longer preheating time to allow the grains to soak up the liquid and expand, making a lighter, more aerated loaf.

fast/rapid bake

On some models this programme can take as little as one hour, which is useful when you have run out of bread and need some fairly quickly. Unlike all other programmes the water (or other liquid) is added warm to activate the yeast quickly and accelerate rising. Because the rising time is so short more yeast is used. The texture of these loaves is more dense and less aerated, but the bread

still has a good flavour. On most machines this programme has only one crust option.

sweet

This programme is used for cakes and breads that contain a high proportion of sugar. It cooks at a slightly lower temperature to stop the sugar burning.

cake

Use this programme for yeast-free breads, teabreads and cakes. Most machines include a mixing cycle, so all you need to do is put the ingredients into the pan and let the machine do the rest, which is ideal if your conventional oven is already in use. Because different models have different baking times, test to see if the cake is ready at the time suggested in the recipe rather than leaving it to the end of the programme by which time the cake might be overcooked. Test by

piercing the centre of the cake with a skewer: it should come out clean. Some bread-making machines don't incorporate a mixing cycle in the cake programme, in which case you'll need to mix the cake ingredients conventionally, remove the kneading blade and turn the blended mixture into the baking pan. Check with the manual first.

dough

This is a really useful programme if you want to give your breads a personal touch by shaping, second proving and baking them conventionally. It's also useful for breads to which you're adding a large amount of additional ingredients that would prevent a good rise if baked in the machine. The dough programme is great for pizza bases, focaccia, sweet buns and teacakes. You don't need to remove the dough from the machine as soon as the programme finishes, but don't leave it too long or the dough might rise up over the top of the pan.

other features
raisin beep

On most models, the programmes have a 'raisin beep', which indicates when you should add additional ingredients, such as dried fruit, cheese, nuts, herbs, seeds and so on, that you wouldn't want to get broken up during kneading. On some machines, whether you're baking bread or using the dough programme, you'll need to select the 'raisin beep' mode, as the machine won't automatically beep. Some models incorporate a raisin/nut dispenser

that can be filled beforehand, so the ingredients are automatically dispensed into the dough at the appropriate point in the programme. If your machine doesn't have this facility, the additional ingredients can be added towards the end of the kneading cycle. Most manuals will provide a chart of how long the different cycles last, so if you're not in the kitchen you can set a timer to remind you when to add additional ingredients.

crust colour

The choice of pale, medium or dark crust is a matter of personal preference. Select the appropriate setting before pressing 'start'.

timer delay

This programme gives you the choice of having freshly baked bread ready for you in the morning, after work or a time that suits you.

Do not use perishable ingredients, such as milk, yogurt and eggs. Consult the manual for selecting time delay options.

loaf size
Most bread-making machines offer three bread sizes:

- small — 500 g (1 lb)
- large — 750 g (1½ lb)
- extra-large — 1 kg (2 lb)

Most of the recipes in this book are for 750 g (1½ lb) loaves, and you should select this setting on the control panel before pressing 'start' because the programme times vary slightly, depending on the size chosen.

keep warm
Most programmes have a keep-warm facility, circulating hot air for a further 30–60 minutes after the bread is baked.

For best results remove the loaf as soon as it's baked or at least within the keep-warm time. After this condensation will form inside the machine and the bread will soften.

adding ingredients
The ingredients should always be added to the bread machine in the order specified in the manual for your particular model, because adding them in the wrong order can result in failure. In most machines it's liquids first, then the flour, yeast and sugar, but in some it's the other way round, with liquids added last. The order the ingredients are added is particularly important when the timer delay is used or the machine has a 'rest' period before the kneading cycle starts, so that the yeast is kept separate from the liquids.

tips for success
- Always measure the ingredients accurately. The wrong quantities of yeast, liquids or solids will result in a poor loaf. Yeast measurements should be level, while liquids measured in a jug should be read at eye level.
- Take the pan out of the machine when you are adding the initial ingredients.
- When you are trying a new recipe check the consistency of the dough after a few minutes kneading. At this stage you can add (cautiously) a dash more liquid if the dough is dry and the flour is sticking around the edges of the pan or, if it's very wet, a little more flour.

- Extra flavourings that you want to remain in pieces, such as raisins and other dried fruits, roasted vegetables, olives and fruit, are best added when the 'raisin beep' sounds. If you add them at the beginning of the programme they may get crushed and their texture and flavour could spoil.
- Use a plastic spatula to scrape down any dry dough that clings to the sides of the pan. Never use a knife or metal implement in the pan because you will damage the nonstick lining.
- Resist the temptation to open the lid once the programme gets going. The draught of cold air will slow down the rising or baking and might result in a sunken loaf. Some of the recipes, however, do suggest brushing with milk just before baking and then closing the lid gently.
- Not all loaves have a domed crust after baking. Some enriched doughs, as well as low-gluten or gluten-free breads, often have a level crust or are slightly sunken.
- The kneading blade often comes out of the tin with the bread when you are shaking it out on to your working surface. Remove the blade as soon as it's cool enough to handle. If the blade remains stuck in position in the pan add a little water to the pan and leave it to soak for 5 minutes by which time the blade should be easy to remove. Don't put the bread pan in the dishwasher. Wash in warm, soapy water and avoid scouring pads, which will damage the nonstick lining.

- If there's a power cut or the machine is accidentally turned off during the programme, turn the machine back on and the programme should start again. If it's switched off for a long time, you might need to start again or finish baking the bread by hand.
- Remember that when you are removing cooked bread from the machine it's as if you were lifting it from the oven, and you'll need to wear oven gloves.
- Conventional bread recipes cannot be made in a bread-making machine because they contain a different proportion of yeast, flour and liquids. Most conventional dough recipes can, however, be followed successfully, provided there's not so much dough that it rises up over the top of the pan.
- Breads made in a bread machine, particularly the more basic recipes, do not keep well and are best eaten on the day they are made.

basic breads

simple white loaf

Makes **1 large loaf**

Time **3–4 hours**, depending
on machine

275 ml (9 fl oz) **water**
30 g (1¼ oz) **unsalted butter**,
softened
1 teaspoon **salt**
475 g (15 oz) **strong white
bread flour**, plus extra
for dusting
2 teaspoons **caster sugar**
1¼ teaspoons **fast-action
dried yeast**

Lift the bread pan out of the machine and fit the blade.
Put the ingredients in the pan, following the order
specified in the manual.

Fit the pan into the machine and close the lid. Set to
a 750 g (1½ lb) loaf size on the basic white
programme. Select your preferred crust setting.

At the end of the programme lift the pan out of the
machine and shake the bread out on to a wire rack.
Dust the top with a little extra flour and leave to cool.

For seeded cottage loaf, put 300 ml (½ pint) water,
2 tablespoons sunflower oil, 1½ teaspoons salt,
3 tablespoons each of sesame seeds, sunflower
seeds and linseeds, 475 g (15 oz) strong white
bread flour, 1 teaspoon caster sugar and 1¼
teaspoons fast-action dried yeast in the bread pan,
following the order specified in the manual. Fit the pan
into the machine and close the lid. Set to the dough
programme. At the end of the programme turn the
dough out on to a floured surface and cut off one
quarter. Shape both pieces of dough into rounds and
place the larger one on a greased baking sheet. Place
the smaller round on top and push a floured wooden
spoon handle down through both doughs. Cover
loosely with oiled clingfilm and leave to rise in a warm
place until almost doubled in size. Bake in a preheated
oven, 220°C (425°F), Gas Mark 7, for 25 minutes until
golden. Transfer to a wire rack to cool.

oatmeal & buttermilk bread

Makes **1 large loaf**

Time **3–4 hours**, depending on machine

125 ml (4 fl oz) **water**

175 ml (6 fl oz) **buttermilk**

1½ teaspoons **salt**

425 g (14 oz) **strong white bread flour**

50 g (2 oz) fine or medium **oatmeal**, plus extra for sprinkling

1½ teaspoons **caster sugar**

1¼ teaspoons **fast-action dried yeast**

milk, to brush

Lift the bread pan out of the machine and fit the blade. Put the ingredients in the pan, following the order specified in the manual.

Fit the pan into the machine and close the lid. Set to a 750 g (1½ lb) loaf size on the basic white programme. Select your preferred crust setting.

Just before baking begins brush the top of the dough lightly with milk and sprinkle with extra oatmeal. Close the lid gently.

At the end of the programme lift the pan out of the machine and shake the bread out on to a wire rack to cool.

For French toast with yogurt, strawberries & honey, cut 4 thick slices of bread. Beat 2 eggs on a plate with 3 tablespoons milk. Turn the bread slices in the milk and leave to soak for 5 minutes. Sprinkle 2 tablespoons caster sugar on to a plate and mix with ¼ teaspoon ground cinnamon. Heat 15 g (½ oz) unsalted butter in a large frying pan with 1 tablespoon mild olive oil and gently fry the bread slices, turning once, until golden on both sides. Turn lightly in the spiced sugar and serve topped with Greek yogurt, strawberries and honey.

granary bread

Makes **1 large loaf**

Time **3½–5 hours**, depending on machine

300 ml (½ pint) **water**

30 g (1¼ oz) **unsalted butter**, softened

1½ teaspoons **salt**

500 g (1 lb) **granary flour**

1 tablespoon **brown sugar**

1¼ teaspoons **fast-action dried yeast**

Lift the bread pan out of the machine and fit the blade. Put the ingredients in the pan, following the order specified in the manual.

Fit the pan into the machine and close the lid. Set to a 750 g (1½ lb) loaf size on the wholemeal programme. Select your preferred crust setting.

At the end of the programme lift the pan out of the machine and shake the bread out on to a wire rack to cool.

For fast-baked double wheat bread, put 275 ml (9 fl oz) warm milk, 25 g (1 oz) soft butter, 2 tablespoons salt, 250 g (8 oz) strong white bread flour, 225 g (7½ oz) wholemeal spelt flour, 2½ teaspoons fast-action dried yeast and 1 teaspoon sugar in the bread pan, following the order specified in the manual. Set to a 750 g (1½ lb) loaf size on the fast/rapid bake programme.

speedy sesame bread

Makes **1 large loaf**
Time **1–2 hours**, depending
  on machine

275 ml (9 fl oz) warm **water**
2 tablespoons **sunflower oil**
1 teaspoon **salt**
2 tablespoons **milk powder**
2 tablespoons **sesame seeds**
475 g (15 oz) **strong white
  bread flour**
1 tablespoon **caster sugar**
2½ teaspoons **fast-action
  dried yeast**

To finish
melted **butter**, to brush
sesame seeds, for sprinkling

Lift the bread pan out of the machine and fit the blade. Put the dough ingredients in the pan, following the order specified in the manual.

Fit the pan into the machine and close the lid. Set to a 750 g (1½ lb) loaf size on the fast/rapid bake programme.

At the end of the programme lift the pan out of the machine and shake the bread out on to a wire rack. Brush the top of the loaf with the butter and sprinkle with a few extra sesame seeds. Brown under the grill, if liked.

For speedy three grain bread, omit the milk powder and sesame seeds from the above recipe and reduce the sugar to 1½ teaspoons. Replace 175 g (6 oz) of the white flour with malted bread flour and a further 50 g (2 oz) with purple wheat flakes. Just before baking begins lightly brush the top of the dough with milk and scatter with extra wheat flakes. Close the lid gently and complete the programme.

ciabatta

Makes **2 loaves**

Time **2–3 hours**, depending on machine, plus standing, shaping, proving and baking

Starter

150 ml (¼ pint) warm **water**

125 g (4 oz) **strong white bread flour**

¼ teaspoon **caster sugar**

½ teaspoon **fast-action dried yeast**

To finish

225 ml (7½ fl oz) **water**

2 tablespoons **olive oil**

1½ teaspoons **salt**

375 g (12 oz) **strong white bread flour**, plus extra for dusting

1½ teaspoons **caster sugar**

1 teaspoon **fast-action dried yeast**

Lift the bread pan out of the machine and fit the blade. Put the starter ingredients in the pan, following the order specified in the manual.

Fit the pan into the machine and close the lid. Set to the dough programme. Turn off the machine before the second kneading cycle and leave the dough to stand for at least 4 hours.

Lift the bread pan out of the machine and add the remaining ingredients. Return to the machine and set to the dough programme.

At the end of the programme turn the dough out on to a floured surface and cut it in half. (The dough will be very sticky.) Using well-floured hands, gently pull the dough into 2 loaves, each about 28 cm (11 inches) long. Place them on a greased and floured baking sheet. Leave in a warm place, uncovered, for about 30 minutes or until it is about half as big again.

Bake in a preheated oven, 220°C (425°F), Gas Mark 7, for about 20 minutes until golden and the loaves sound hollow when tapped with the fingertips. Transfer to a wire rack to cool. Dust with flour.

For sun-dried tomato & herb ciabatta, drain and thinly slice 75 g (3 oz) sun-dried tomatoes in olive oil. Roughly chop 15 g (½ oz) fresh mixed herbs (such as basil, parsley, oregano and thyme). Make the dough in the machine as above using olive oil from the tomato jar and adding the sliced tomatoes and herbs when the machine beeps. Turn out on to a floured surface and finish as above.

couronne

Makes **1 loaf**

Time **1½–2½ hours**, depending
on machine, plus shaping,
proving and baking

175 ml (6 fl oz) **water**
200 ml (7 fl oz) **natural yogurt**
1½ teaspoons **salt**
500 g (1 lb) **unbleached
strong white bread flour**,
plus extra for sprinkling
2 teaspoons **caster sugar**
1¼ teaspoons **fast-action
dried yeast**

Lift the bread pan out of the machine and fit the blade.
Put the ingredients in the pan, following the order
specified in the manual.

Fit the pan into the machine and close the lid. Set to
the dough programme.

At the end of the programme turn the dough out on
to a floured surface and shape into a round, then
make a small hole in the centre with your fingertips.
Enlarge the hole with your fist until it is about 12 cm
(5 inches) across and the dough ring is about 20 cm
(8 inches) across.

Transfer the bread to a greased baking sheet and make
3–4 cuts across the surface (if liked). Grease the base
of a small basin and put it in the centre of the dough to
keep the hole intact. Cover both dough and basin with
lightly oiled clingfilm and leave in a warm place for
about 30 minutes or until it is half as big again.

Remove the clingfilm and basin, sprinkle the dough
with flour and bake in a preheated oven, 220°C (420°F),
Gas Mark 7, for 20–25 minutes until it is well risen and
browned and the bread sounds hollow when tapped
with the fingertips. Cover with foil after 15 minutes if
over-browning. Transfer to a wire rack to cool.

For easy sourdough bread, follow the recipe above
using warm water instead of cold and Greek yogurt
instead of natural. Increase the yeast to 2½ teaspoons.
Set to a 750 g (1½ lb) loaf size on the fast/rapid bake
programme. Just before baking begins, sprinkle the
top of the dough with a little extra flour. Close the lid
gently and complete the programme.

walnut & honey bread

Makes **1 large loaf**
Time **3½–5 hours**, depending
on machine

100 g (3½ oz) **walnut pieces**
350 ml (12 fl oz) **water**
3 tablespoons **clear honey**,
plus extra to drizzle
40 g (1½ oz) **unsalted butter**,
softened
1½ teaspoons **salt**
350 g (11½ oz) **strong
wholemeal bread flour**
150 g (5 oz) **strong white
bread flour**
1¼ teaspoons **fast-action
dried yeast**

Lightly toast the walnuts either in a frying pan over
a gentle heat or under the grill.

Lift the bread pan out of the machine and fit the blade.
Put the ingredients, except the walnuts, in the pan,
following the order specified in the manual.

Fit the pan into the machine and close the lid. Set to
a 750 g (1½ lb) loaf size on the wholemeal programme.
Select your preferred crust setting. Add the walnuts
when the machine beeps.

At the end of the programme lift the pan out of the
machine and shake the bread out on to a wire rack
to cool. Serve drizzled with extra honey.

For mini pecan & maple loaves, lightly toast 100 g
(3½ oz) roughly chopped pecan nuts. Make the bread
as above, using the pecans instead of the walnuts and
replacing the honey with 3 tablespoons maple syrup.
Use the dough programme, cut the dough into
8 pieces and press into 8 greased 200 ml (7 fl oz)
individual loaf tins. Cover loosely with oiled clingfilm
and leave to rise in a warm place for 30 minutes.
Brush with a little maple syrup and bake in a preheated
oven, 220°C (425°F), Gas Mark 7, for about 20 minutes
until well risen and golden. Serve drizzled with extra
maple syrup.

mixed seed bread

Makes **1 large loaf**
Time **3½–5 hours**, depending
    on machine

Dough
300 ml (½ pint) **water**
30 g (1¼ oz) **unsalted butter**,
    softened
1½ teaspoons **salt**
3 tablespoons **sesame seeds**
3 tablespoons **sunflower
    seeds**
3 tablespoons **linseeds**
475 g (15 oz) **malthouse
    flour**
1 tablespoon **brown sugar**
1¼ teaspoons **fast-action
    dried yeast**

To finish
milk, to brush
extra **seeds**, for sprinkling
    (optional)

Lift the bread pan out of the machine and fit the blade. Put the dough ingredients in the pan, following the order specified in the manual.

Fit the pan into the machine and close the lid. Set to a 750 g (1½ lb) loaf size on the wholemeal programme. Select your preferred crust setting.

Just before baking begins brush the top of the dough with a little milk and sprinkle over some extra seeds (if liked). Close the lid gently.

At the end of the programme lift the pan out of the machine, loosen the bread with a spatula if necessary and shake it out on to a wire rack to cool.

For seeded cheese batons, follow the recipe above but finely grate 40 g (1½ oz) extra-mature Cheddar cheese and add to the machine with the flour. Set to the dough programme. At the end of the programme turn the dough out on to a floured surface and cut it into 3 equal pieces. Roll each piece to a sausage, about 28 cm (11 inches) long, transfer to a large, greased baking sheet, leaving enough space around the dough for them to rise. Cover loosely with oiled clingfilm and leave in a warm place for about 30 minutes or until it is about half as big again. Use a floured knife to make diagonal cuts across the top of each baton and bake in a preheated oven, 200°C (400°F), Gas Mark 6, for 15–20 minutes until risen and golden. Transfer to a wire rack to cool.

boston brown bread

Makes **2 small loaves**

Time **1½–2½ hours**, depending on machine, plus shaping, proving and baking

250 ml (8 fl oz) **milk**

5 tablespoons **molasses syrup**

1 teaspoon **salt**

175 g (6 oz) **strong wholemeal bread flour**

175 g (6 oz) **strong white bread flour**, plus extra for dusting

50 g (2 oz) **rye flour**

50 g (2 oz) **cornmeal**

1¼ teaspoons **fast-action dried yeast**

Lift the bread pan out of the machine and fit the blade. Put the ingredients in the pan, following the order specified in the manual.

Fit the pan into the machine and close the lid. Set to the dough programme. Thoroughly wash 2 empty 800 g (1 lb 10 oz) tomato, new potato or other large cans. Place them on a baking sheet and grease and line the cans as you would a cake tin.

At the end of the programme turn the dough out on to a floured surface and cut it in half. Shape each piece into a ball and drop them into the cans. Cover loosely with oiled clingfilm and leave to rise in a warm place for about 40 minutes or until the dough reaches the top of the cans.

Bake in a preheated oven, 200°C (400°F), Gas Mark 6, for 25 minutes. Remove from the cans and tap the bases. If the bread sounds hollow it is cooked, if not return to the oven for a little longer (but don't fit them back in the tins). Transfer to a wire rack. Dust the top lightly with a little extra white bread flour and leave to cool.

For fruited Boston bread, roughly chop 75 g (3 oz) pitted dates or prunes. Make the bread using the wholemeal programme, 750 g (1½ lb) loaf size and preferred crust setting. Add the dates or prunes when the machine beeps.

breakfast muesli bread

Makes **1 extra-large loaf**
Time **3–4 hours**, depending
  on machine

300 ml (½ pint) **apple juice**
1 large **egg**, beaten
25 g (1 oz) **unsalted butter**,
  softened
1½ teaspoons **salt**
2 tablespoons **milk powder**
1 teaspoon **ground mixed
  spice**
125 g (4 oz) **fruit muesli**, plus
  extra for sprinkling
425 g (13 oz) **strong white
  bread flour**
50 g (2 oz) **light muscovado
  sugar**
1¼ teaspoons **fast-action
  dried yeast**
50 g (2 oz) **raisins**
milk, to brush

Lift the bread pan out of the machine and fit the blade.
Put the ingredients, except the raisins, in the pan
following the order specified in the manual.

Fit the pan into the machine and close the lid. Set to
a 1 kg (2 lb) loaf size on the basic white programme.
Select your preferred crust setting. Add the raisins
when the machine beeps.

Just before baking begins brush the top of the dough
lightly with milk and sprinkle with a little muesli. Close
the lid gently.

At the end of the programme lift the pan out of the
machine, loosen the bread with a spatula if necessary
and shake it out on to a wire rack to cool.

For fresh blueberry conserve, to accompany the
bread, blend 1 teaspoon cornflour with 1 tablespoon
water in a small saucepan. Add 100 ml (3½ fl oz)
apple or orange juice, 3 tablespoons caster sugar
and ½ teaspoon vanilla extract. Heat gently, stirring,
until slightly thickened. Tip in 200 g (7 oz) fresh or
frozen blueberries and cook gently for 1–2 minutes
until the blueberries soften and start to burst. Serve
warm or cold, spooned over the bread and topped
with Greek yogurt.

fast-baked rye & caraway bread

Makes **1 large loaf**
Time **1–2 hours**, depending
  on machine

200 ml (7 fl oz) warm **water**
200 ml (7 fl oz) **Greek yogurt**
1½ teaspoons **salt**
1 tablespoon **caraway seeds**
325 g (11 oz) **strong white
  bread flour**
175 g (6 oz) **rye flour**
1 tablespoon **caster sugar**
2½ teaspoons **fast-action
  dried yeast**

Lift the bread pan out of the machine and fit the blade. Put the ingredients in the pan, following the order specified in the manual.

Fit the pan into the machine and close the lid. Set to a 750 g (1½ lb) loaf size on the fast/rapid bake programme.

At the end of the programme lift the pan out of the machine and shake the bread out on to a wire rack to cool. Serve thinly sliced.

For toasted rye & smoked trout sandwich, mix 50 g (2 oz) cream cheese with 75 g (3 oz) skinned and boned smoked trout and 1 finely chopped spring onion. Mix 1 tablespoon chilli-infused oil with ¼ teaspoon caster sugar and 1 teaspoon wine vinegar. Lightly toast 2 slices of rye bread and sandwich with the trout mixture, a handful of watercress leaves and the dressing.

brioche

Makes **1 loaf**
Time **1½–2½ hours**, depending
  on machine, plus shaping,
  proving and baking

3 **eggs**, beaten
75 g (3 oz) **unsalted butter**,
  softened
¼ teaspoon **salt**
250 g (8 oz) **strong white
  bread flour**
25 g (1 oz) **caster sugar**
1 teaspoon **fast-action dried
  yeast**
egg yolk, to glaze

Lift the bread pan out of the machine and fit the blade.
Put the ingredients in the pan, following the order
specified in the manual.

Fit the pan into the machine and close the lid. Set to
the dough programme. Thoroughly butter a 750 ml
(1¼ pint) brioche mould or a 1 kg (2 lb) loaf tin.

At the end of the programme turn the dough out on
to a floured surface and cut off one quarter. Shape the
larger piece into a ball and drop it into the brioche tin.
Push a deep, wide hole into the dough with your fingers.
Shape the remaining dough into a ball and press it
gently into the indented top. (If you are using a loaf tin
shape the dough into an oval and drop it into the tin.)

Cover loosely with oiled clingfilm and leave to rise in a
warm place for 50–60 minutes or until almost doubled
in size. Mix the egg yolk with 1 tablespoon water and
gently brush over the dough. Bake in a preheated oven,
220°C (425°F), Gas Mark 7, for 20–25 minutes or until
deep golden and firm. (Cover the loaf with foil if the
crust starts to over-brown.)

After baking leave the bread in the tin for a few
minutes, then shake out on to a wire rack to cool.

For baby chocolate brioche buns, make the dough as
above and divide it into 8 pieces. Push 15 g (½ oz) plain
dark chocolate into the centre of each piece and seal
the dough around the chocolate. Space the buns well
apart on a greased baking sheet. Cover loosely with
oiled clingfilm and leave to rise in a warm place until
almost doubled in size. Glaze and bake as above,
reducing the cooking time to about 15 minutes.

date & malted barley bread

Makes **1 large loaf**

Time **2¾–3½ hours**, depending on machine

250 ml (8 fl oz) **milk**, plus 1 tablespoon to brush

5 tablespoons **date syrup** or **malted barley extract**

25 g (1 oz) **unsalted butter**, softened

1 teaspoon **salt**

325 g (11 oz) **barley flour**

150 g (5 oz) **strong white bread flour**

1¼ teaspoons **fast-action dried yeast**

150 g (5 oz) pitted **dates**, chopped

barley flakes, for sprinkling (optional)

Lift the bread pan out of the machine and fit the blade. Put the ingredients, except the dates, in the pan, following the order specified in the manual.

Fit the pan into the machine and set to a 750 g (1½ lb) loaf size on the sweet programme (or the wholemeal programme if the machine doesn't have a sweet setting). Add the dates when the machine beeps.

Just before baking begins brush the top of the dough lightly with milk and sprinkle with barley flakes (if liked). Close the lid gently.

At the end of the programme lift the pan out of the machine and shake the bread out on to a wire rack to cool. Serve buttered with breakfast preserve or honey, if liked.

For spiced fruit loaves, add 2 teaspoons ground mixed spice with the flours and set to the dough programme, adding 150 g (5 oz) chopped pitted prunes or chopped dried figs (instead of the dates) when the machine beeps. At the end of the programme turn the dough out on to a floured surface and cut it in half. Shape each half into an oval and drop into 2 greased 500 g (1 lb) loaf tins. Cover loosely with oiled clingfilm and leave to rise in a warm place for 30–40 minutes or until almost doubled in size. Bake in a preheated oven, 220°C (425°F), Gas Mark 7, for 20–25 minutes. Turn out of the tins on to a wire rack to cool.

yogurt, honey & fennel seed bread

Makes **1 extra-large loaf**

Time **3–4 hours**, depending on machine

200 ml (7 fl oz) **water**

150 ml (5 fl oz) **Greek yogurt**

4 tablespoons **set honey**

30 g (1¼ oz) **unsalted butter**, softened

½ teaspoon **salt**

2 tablespoons **fennel seeds**, roughly crushed

500 g (1 lb) **strong white bread flour**

1¼ teaspoon **fast-action dried yeast**

Lift the bread pan out of the machine and fit the blade. Put the ingredients in the pan, following the order specified in the manual.

Fit the pan into the machine and close the lid. Set to the 1 kg (2 lb) loaf size on the basic white programme. Select your preferred crust setting.

At the end of the programme lift the pan out of the machine, loosen the bread with a spatula if necessary and shake it out on to a wire rack to cool.

For panzanella salad, to make using the bread, roast 4 deseeded and roughly sliced peppers in a dash of olive oil until they are beginning to brown. Tear 100 g (3½ oz) bread into bite-sized pieces and scatter them on a foil-lined baking sheet. Drizzle with another 2 tablespoons oil and grill until browned. Quarter 750 g (1½ lb) well-flavoured tomatoes and scoop the seeds into a sieve placed over a bowl. Press the seeds and pulp in the sieve to extract the juice. Put the tomatoes, peppers, bread, a handful of basil leaves, a finely chopped shallot and plenty of black olives into a salad bowl. Whisk the tomato juice with 1 crushed garlic clove, 4 teaspoons wine vinegar and plenty of seasoning. Pour the dressing over the salad and mix well.

cranberry & pomegranate bread

Makes **1 large loaf**

Time **3–4 hours**, depending
on machine

325 ml (11 fl oz) **water**

2 tablespoons **olive oil**

1 teaspoon **salt**

3 tablespoons **dried
pomegranate seeds**

125 g (4 oz) **buckwheat flour**,
plus extra for dusting

375 g (12 oz) **strong white
bread flour**

1 tablespoon **light
muscovado sugar**

1¼ teaspoons **fast-action
dried yeast**

75 g (3 oz) **dried cranberries**

Lift the bread pan out of the machine and fit the blade.
Put the ingredients, except the dried cranberries, in the
pan, following the order specified in the manual.

Fit the pan into the machine and close the lid. Set to
a 750 g (1½ lb) loaf size on the basic white programme.
Select your preferred crust setting. Add the dried
cranberries when the machine beeps.

At the end of the programme lift the pan out of the
machine and shake the bread out on to a wire rack.
Dust the top lightly with a little extra buckwheat flour
and leave to cool. Slice and serve with cream cheese
and fruit compote, if liked.

For buckwheat, linseed & apricot bread, lightly
crush 4 tablespoons linseeds using a coffee grinder
reserved for crushing seeds and spices (or use the
small bowl of a food processor). Make the bread as
above, adding ½ teaspoon cinnamon with the flour.
Use the linseeds instead of the pomegranate seeds
and 100 g (3½ oz) chopped dried apricots instead of
the cranberries.

savoury
breads

mushroom & mozzarella stromboli

Makes **1 loaf**
(about 8 thick slices)
Time **1½–2½ hours**, depending
on machine, plus shaping,
proving and baking

Dough
225 ml (7½ fl oz) **water**
3 tablespoons extra-virgin
olive oil
1 teaspoon **salt**
400 g (13 oz) **strong white
bread flour**
1 teaspoon **fast-action dried
yeast**

To finish
250 g (8 oz) **chestnut
mushrooms**, thinly sliced
3 tablespoons extra-virgin
olive oil
300 g (10 oz) **mozzarella
cheese**, sliced
25 g (1 oz) **basil leaves**
2 teaspoons **green
peppercorns** in brine, rinsed
and drained
sea salt, for sprinkling

Lift the bread pan out of the machine and fit the blade. Put the dough ingredients in the pan, following the order specified in the manual. Fit the pan into the machine and close the lid. Set to the dough programme.

Meanwhile, fry the mushrooms in 2 tablespoons oil until golden. Leave to cool.

At the end of the programme turn the dough out on to a floured surface and roll it out to a 33 cm (13 inch) square. Arrange the mozzarella slices, basil leaves and mushrooms over the dough. Lightly crush the peppercorns and scatter over the filling with a little salt.

Loosely roll up the dough and transfer to a large, greased baking sheet with the join underneath. Pinch the ends together to seal. Cover loosely with oiled clingfilm and leave in a warm place for 30 minutes.

Flour a large skewer or meat fork and pierce the dough all over, making sure you go right through to the baking sheet. Drizzle with the remaining oil and scatter with sea salt. Bake in a preheated oven, 220°C (425°F), Gas Mark 7, for about 25 minutes until risen and golden. Serve warm or cold.

For artichoke & Gruyère stromboli, make the dough as above. Drain 275 g (9 oz) artichokes in olive oil and roughly chop. Roll out the dough as above and scatter with 200 g (7 oz) grated Gruyère cheese, the artichokes, 6 tablespoons chopped parsley, 2 finely chopped garlic cloves, the grated rind of 1 lemon and seasoning. Finish as above.

sweet dill & mustard loaf

Makes **1 large loaf**
Time **3–4 hours**, depending
  on machine

200 ml (7 fl oz) **water**
150 g (5 oz) **soured cream**
3 tablespoons **grainy
  mustard**
25 g (1 oz) **dill**, chopped
1 teaspoon **salt**
500 g (1 lb) **strong white
  bread flour**
2 tablespoons **caster sugar**
1¼ teaspoons **fast-action
  dried yeast**

Lift the bread pan out of the machine and fit the blade. Put the ingredients in the pan, following the order specified in the manual. Add the mustard and dill with the liquids.

Fit the pan into the machine and close the lid. Set to a 750 g (1½ lb) loaf size on the basic white programme. Select your preferred crust setting.

At the end of the programme lift the pan out of the machine and shake the bread out on to a wire rack to cool.

For creamy smoked salmon pâté, to serve with the freshly baked bread, roughly chop 200 g (7 oz) smoked salmon trimmings and put in a food processor. Add 25 g (1 oz) butter, melted and cooled, 1 tablespoon lemon juice, 100 g (3½ oz) cream cheese and plenty of black pepper. Blend until smooth, scraping down any pieces that cling to the sides of the bowl. Transfer to a small serving dish and chill until ready to serve.

chilli & smoked paprika bread

Makes **1 large loaf**
Time **3–4 hours**, depending
on machine

275 ml (9 fl oz) **water**
2 tablespoons **olive oil**
1 teaspoon **salt**
1 teaspoon **smoked paprika**
1 large mild fresh **red chilli**,
halved, deseeded and finely
chopped
300 g (10 oz) **strong white
bread flour**
150 g (5 oz) **strong
wholemeal flour**
1 teaspoon **caster sugar**
1¼ teaspoons **fast-action
dried yeast**
50 g (2 oz) **sun-dried
tomatoes** in oil, drained and
roughly chopped (optional)

Lift the bread pan out of the machine and fit the blade.
Put the ingredients, except the sun-dried tomatoes, in
the pan following the order specified in the manual.

Fit the pan into the machine and close the lid. Set to a
750 g (1½ lb) loaf size on the basic white programme.
Select your preferred crust setting. Add the sun-dried
tomatoes (if using) when the machine beeps.

At the end of the programme lift the pan out of the
machine and shake the bread out on to a wire rack
to cool.

For spicy peanut & chilli loaf, omit the smoked
paprika and sun-dried tomatoes from the recipe.
Use sesame oil instead of olive oil and add 75 g
(3 oz) crunchy peanut butter and 25 g (1 oz) grated
firm creamed coconut. Add 2 finely chopped spring
onions when the machine beeps. Just before baking
begins brush the top of the dough with milk and
sprinkle with mild chilli powder. Close the lid gently
and complete the programme.

spicy slipper breads

Makes **4 loaves**

Time **1½–2½ hours**, depending on machine, plus shaping, proving and baking

Dough

200 ml (7 fl oz) **water**

3 tablespoons **olive oil**

1 teaspoon **salt**

1 tablespoon **cumin seeds**, lightly crushed

1 teaspoon **ground cinnamon**

300 g (10 oz) **strong white bread flour**

100 g (3½ oz) **chickpea flour**

1 tablespoon **caster sugar**

1¼ teaspoons **fast-action dried yeast**

To finish

5 tablespoons **olive oil**

2 **onions**, thinly sliced

3 **garlic cloves**, crushed

400 g (13 oz) can **chickpeas**, rinsed and drained

1 tablespoon chopped **mint**

4 tablespoons chopped **coriander**

1 tablespoon **lemon juice**

250 g (8 oz) **haloumi cheese**, diced

salt and **black pepper**

Lift the bread pan out of the machine and fit the blade. Put the dough ingredients in the pan, following the order specified in the manual. Add the seeds with the flours. Fit the pan into the machine and close the lid. Set to the dough programme.

Heat 3 tablespoons olive oil in a pan and fry the onions for 10 minutes. Add the garlic, then the chickpeas, mint, coriander, lemon juice and seasoning.

At the end of the programme turn the dough out on to a floured surface and divide it into 4 pieces. Roll each into an oval, about 22 x 16 cm (8½ x 6½ inches), and place on a large, greased baking sheet. Stir the cheese into the chickpea mixture and scatter over the dough. Fold the dough over the filling so the filling is still visible. Cover with oiled clingfilm and leave in a warm place to rise for 30 minutes or until it is half as big again.

Lightly score the dough with a floured knife and drizzle with the remaining olive oil. Sprinkle with salt and bake in a preheated oven, 220°C (425°F), Gas Mark 7, for about 20 minutes until slightly risen and golden. Serve warm.

For spicy chickpea & onion loaf, fry 1 finely chopped small red onion in 1 tablespoon olive oil with 1 tablespoon lightly crushed cumin seeds and 1 teaspoon ground cinnamon. Put in the bread pan with 200 ml (7 fl oz) water, 3 tablespoons olive oil, 1 teaspoon salt, 300 g (10 oz) strong white bread flour, 100 g (3½ oz) chickpea flour, 1 tablespoon caster sugar and 1 teaspoon fast-action dried yeast, in the order given in the manual. (Add the onions with the liquids.) Set to a 750 g (1½ lb) loaf size on the basic white programme.

fennel, bacon & gruyère twist

Makes **1 large loaf** (about
8 thick slices)
Time **1½–2½ hours**, depending
on machine, plus shaping,
proving and baking

Dough
200 ml (7 fl oz) **milk**
2 **garlic cloves**, crushed
50 g (2 oz) **unsalted butter**,
softened
1 teaspoon **salt**
350 g (11½ oz) **strong white
bread flour**
1 teaspoon **caster sugar**
1 teaspoon **fast-action dried
yeast**

To finish
2 tablespoons **olive oil**
125 g (4 oz) **smoked streaky
bacon**, chopped
1 **fennel bulb**, chopped
2 teaspoons **fennel seeds**,
lightly crushed, plus extra for
sprinkling
175 g (6 oz) **Gruyère cheese**,
grated
black pepper

Lift the bread pan from the machine and fit the blade.
Put the dough ingredients in the pan, following the order
specified in the manual. Add the garlic with the milk.

Fit the pan into the machine and close the lid. Set to
the dough programme.

Heat the oil in a frying pan and gently fry the bacon,
fennel and fennel seeds for 10 minutes until softened
and golden. Leave to cool.

At the end of the programme turn the dough out on to
a floured surface and roll it out to a rectangle, about
38 x 30 cm (15 x 12 inches). Scatter the bacon and
fennel mixture over the dough to about 2 cm (¾ inch)
from the edges. Sprinkle all but 15 g (½ oz) of the
Gruyère on top and season with plenty of pepper.

Loosely roll up the dough, starting from a short side,
and place on a large, greased baking sheet with the
join underneath. Lift one end and twist the dough to
create a corkscrew effect. Repeat at the other end.
Cover with oiled clingfilm and leave to rise in a warm
place until nearly doubled in size.

Sprinkle the remaining cheese on top and sprinkle with
extra seeds. Bake in a preheated oven, 220°C (425°F),
Gas Mark 7, for 25 minutes until risen and golden.

For tapenade & tomato twist, make the dough as
above, adding 2 teaspoons chopped thyme. Spread
the dough with 6 tablespoons black olive tapenade
and scatter with 200 g (7 oz) halved cherry tomatoes.
Season with plenty of black pepper, then roll up and
finish as above.

chilli chocolate bread

Makes **1 large loaf**
Time **3–4 hours**, depending
  on machine

250 ml (8 fl oz) **water**
3 tablespoons **sunflower oil**
1½ teaspoons **salt**
1½ teaspoons crushed **dried
  chillies**
½ teaspoon **ground cinnamon**
75 g (3 oz) **plain dark
  chocolate** (85% cocoa
  solids), grated
1 tablespoon **cocoa powder**
350 g (11½ oz) **strong white
  bread flour**
50 g (2 oz) **cornmeal**
2 tablespoons **molasses
  sugar**
1 teaspoon **fast-action dried
  yeast**

Lift the bread pan out of the machine and fit the blade. Put the ingredients in the pan, following the order specified in the manual. Add the spices, grated chocolate and cocoa powder with the flour.

Fit the pan into the machine and close the lid. Set to a 750 g (1½ lb) loaf size on the basic white programme. Select your preferred crust setting.

At the end of the programme lift the pan out of the machine and shake the bread out on to a wire rack to cool.

For spicy chicken mole with chilli bread, make the bread as above, omitting the chocolate and cocoa powder and adding an extra 25 g (1 oz) white bread flour. Leave to cool. Dust 4 halved chicken legs with 1 tablespoon lightly crushed cumin seeds and seasoning. Fry in 2 tablespoons vegetable oil in a flameproof casserole until golden. Add 1 large chopped onion and 2 crushed garlic cloves and fry for a further 5 minutes. In a food processor blend 40 g (1½ oz) blanched almonds with 2 tablespoons sesame seeds and 15 g (½ oz) crumbled white bread until ground. Add 450 ml (¾ pint) hot chicken stock and add to the chicken with 15 g (½ oz) dark chocolate, a handful of chopped fresh coriander and seasoning. Bring to the boil, cover with a lid and cook in a preheated oven, 200°C (400°F), Gas Mark 6, for 50 minutes. Serve slices of the chilli bread with the mole.

olive oil, rosemary & raisin bread

Makes **1 large loaf**

Time **1½–2½ hours**, depending on machine, plus shaping, proving and baking

325 ml (11 fl oz) **water**

100 ml (3½ fl oz) extra-virgin **olive oil**

2 teaspoons **sea salt**, plus extra for sprinkling

2 tablespoons **milk powder**

2 teaspoons **fennel seeds**, lightly crushed

1 tablespoon chopped **rosemary**

600 g (1 lb 3 oz) **strong white bread flour**

1 tablespoon **caster sugar**

2 teaspoons **fast-action dried yeast**

100 g (3 oz) **raisins**

rosemary sprigs, to garnish

Lift the bread pan out of the machine and fit the blade. Put the ingredients, except the raisins, in the pan, following the order specified in the manual. Add the seeds and rosemary with the flour.

Fit the pan into the machine and close the lid. Set to the dough programme, adding the raisins when the machine beeps.

At the end of the programme turn the dough out on to a floured surface and shape it into a round. Make a hole through the centre of the loaf with your fingertips, then enlarge it with your hand until the dough is ring-shaped with a hole 10 cm (4 inches) in diameter in the middle. Put the dough on a large, greased baking sheet, cover loosely with oiled clingfilm and leave to rise in a warm place for about 45 minutes or until it has almost doubled in size.

Score the dough at intervals with a floured knife and scatter with rosemary sprigs and sea salt. Bake in a preheated oven, 220°C (425°F), Gas Mark 7, for 40 minutes until risen and golden. Cover the bread with foil and replace the rosemary sprigs if they start to over-brown.

For Mediterranean herb bread, make the dough as above using 2 teaspoons dried oregano instead of the rosemary and omitting the raisins. Add 25 g (1 oz) torn basil leaves and 3 tablespoons capers, drained and dried, when the machine beeps. Finish as above, without the rosemary sprigs.

beer & brown sugar bread

Makes **1 large loaf**

Time **3½–5 hours**, depending
on machine

Dough

200 ml (7 fl oz) **Guinness** or
strong brown beer

100 ml (3½ fl oz) cold **water**

2 tablespoons **sunflower oil**

1 teaspoon **salt**

100 g (3½ oz) **rye flour**

375 g (12 oz) **strong granary
flour**

2 tablespoons **dark
muscovado sugar**

1¼ teaspoons **fast-action
dried yeast**

To finish

1 tablespoon **milk**, to brush

1 tablespoon **poppy seeds**,
for sprinkling

Lift the bread pan out of the machine and fit the blade.
Put the dough ingredients in the pan, following the
order specified in the manual.

Fit the pan into the machine and close the lid. Set to a
750 g (1½ lb) loaf size on the wholemeal programme.
Select your preferred crust setting.

Just before baking begins brush the top of the dough
with the milk and sprinkle with the poppy seeds. Close
the lid gently.

At the end of the programme lift the pan out of the
machine and shake the bread out on to a wire rack
to cool. Serve with potted cheese (see below), sliced
apple and grapes, if liked.

For potted cheese, to serve with the bread, crumble
200 g (7 oz) mature Cheddar or Stilton cheese into a
food processor and add 50 g (2 oz) softened butter,
plenty of freshly grated nutmeg and ½ teaspoon
English mustard. Blend lightly. Add 2 tablespoons
snipped chives and blend lightly to mix. Pack into a
small serving dish and chill until ready to serve. If liked,
seal the cheese with clarified butter to stop it drying
out. Melt 50 g (2 oz) butter in a small saucepan and
let the butter stand for a couple of minutes so the
sediment settles on the base. Spoon the clear butter
over the cheese and chill.

onion & tomato schiacciata

Makes **1 round loaf**

Time **about 1½–2½ hours**, depending on machine, plus shaping, proving and baking

Dough

275 ml (9 fl oz) **water**

3 tablespoons **olive oil**

1 teaspoon **salt**

475 g (15 oz) **strong white bread flour**

2 teaspoons **caster sugar**

1½ teaspoons **fast-action dried yeast**

To finish

4 tablespoons **olive oil**

1 large **red onion**, thinly sliced

2 **garlic cloves**, finely chopped

1 teaspoon **caster sugar**

3 teaspoons **black olive pesto** or **sun-dried tomato pesto**

50 g (2 oz) **sun-dried tomatoes**, drained and sliced

small bunch of **basil**

coarse salt flakes

Lift the bread pan out of the machine and fit the blade. Put the dough ingredients in the pan, following the order specified in the manual. Fit the pan into the machine and close the lid. Set to the dough programme.

Heat 1 tablespoon oil in a frying pan. Add the onion and garlic and fry gently for 5 minutes until softened. Scoop out one-quarter and reserve for the topping. Add the sugar to the remaining onions and cook for a few minutes more until caramelized.

At the end of the programme turn the dough out on to a floured surface and cut it in half. Roll one half to a 23 cm (9 inch) round. Place on an oiled baking sheet. Spread with the pesto. Top with the caramelized onions, three-quarters of the sun-dried tomatoes, half the basil leaves and drizzle with 2 tablespoons oil.

Roll out the remaining dough to a circle and cover the first circle. Sprinkle with the remaining onions, tomatoes, basil leaves and a little salt. Cover loosely with oiled clingfilm and leave to rise in a warm place for 30 minutes.

Bake in a preheated oven, 200°C (400°F), Gas Mark 6, for 25 minutes until golden brown and the centre is cooked through. Transfer to a chopping board, drizzle with the remaining oil and serve warm, cut into wedges.

For homemade sun-dried tomato pesto, drain the oil from 125 g (4 oz) sun-dried tomatoes and finely chop in a food processor with 25 g (1 oz) pine nuts, 10 chopped black olives and 2 chopped garlic cloves. Add 5 tablespoons olive oil and 25 g (1 oz) grated Parmesan cheese. Season lightly.

irish black bread

Makes **1 large loaf**

Time **3–4 hours**, depending on machine

300 ml (½ pint) **Guinness or stout**

25 g (1 oz) **unsalted butter**, softened

1½ teaspoons **salt**

2 teaspoons **ground ginger**

275 g (9 oz) **strong white bread flour**

175 g (6 oz) **strong wholemeal flour**

3 tablespoons **molasses sugar**

1¼ teaspoons **fast-action dried yeast**

Measure the Guinness into a jug and leave it to settle so that you can accurately gauge the level.

Lift the bread pan out of the machine and fit the blade. Put the ingredients in the pan, following the order specified in the manual. Add the ginger with the flour.

Fit the pan into the machine and close the lid. Set to a 750 g (1½ lb) loaf size on the basic white programme. Select your preferred crust setting.

At the end of the programme lift the pan out of the machine and shake the bread out on to a wire rack to cool.

olive & tomato bread

Makes **1 large loaf**

Time **1½–2½ hours**, depending on machine, plus shaping, proving and baking

Dough

275 ml (9 fl oz) **water**

2 tablespoons **olive oil**

1 teaspoon **salt**

475 g (15 oz) **strong white bread flour**

1 teaspoon **caster sugar**

1¼ teaspoons **fast-action dried yeast**

To finish

125 g (4 oz) pitted or stuffed **green olives**, roughly chopped

40 g (1½ oz) **sun-dried tomatoes** (not in oil), roughly chopped

coarse sea salt and **paprika**, for sprinkling

Lift the bread pan out of the machine and fit the blade. Put the dough ingredients in the pan, following the order specified in the manual.

Fit the pan into the machine and close the lid. Set to the dough programme.

At the end of the programme lift the pan out of the machine and turn the dough out on to a floured surface. Gradually work in the chopped olives and tomatoes. Pat the dough into a circle about 20 cm (8 inches) across and use a floured knife to mark it into 8 wedges. Do not cut right through to the base.

Sprinkle the salt and paprika over the dough, transfer to a large, lightly greased backing sheet, cover loosely with oiled clingfilm and leave to rise in a warm place for 30 minutes until it is half as big again.

Bake in a preheated oven, 200°C (400°F), Gas Mark 6, for 30 minutes. Check after 15 minutes and cover with foil if over-browning. Transfer to a wire rack to cool.

For pancetta & Parmesan bread, finely chop 100 g (3½ oz) pancetta. Heat 1 tablespoon olive oil in a small frying pan and fry the pancetta with 1 chopped shallot for 5 minutes until it is beginning to colour. Leave to cool. Make the bread as above, adding the pancetta and shallot and 50 g (2 oz) grated Parmesan cheese to the dough instead of the olives and tomatoes. Finish as above.

pissaladière

Makes **1 large tart**

Time **1½–2½ hours**, depending on machine, plus shaping, proving and baking

Dough

1 large **egg**, beaten

1 tablespoon **olive oil**

½ teaspoon **salt**

250 g (8 oz) **strong white bread flour**

1 tablespoon **caster sugar**

¾ teaspoon **fast-action dried yeast**

To finish

4 tablespoons extra-virgin **olive oil**

625 g (1¼ lb) **onions**, thinly sliced

2 teaspoons chopped **thyme**

50 g (2 oz) can **anchovies** in olive oil

about 10 pitted **black olives**

salt and **black pepper**

thyme sprigs, to garnish

Lift the bread pan out of the machine and fit the blade. Put the egg in a jug and make it up to 150 ml (¼ pint) with water. Put the dough ingredients in the pan, following the order specified in the manual. Fit the pan into the machine and close the lid. Set to the dough programme. Check the dough after 5 minutes' kneading and add 1 tablespoon more water if it feels dry.

Prepare the topping. Heat 2 tablespoons oil in a frying pan and fry the onions for about 20 minutes, stirring frequently. Stir in the thyme and plenty of seasoning.

At the end of the programme turn the dough out on to a floured surface and roll it out thinly to a circle about 33 cm (13 inches) across. Lift it on to a large, greased baking sheet, reshape the circle and make a rim by folding over the edges of the dough and pressing them down firmly. Leave to stand, uncovered, for 10 minutes.

Bake in a preheated oven, 220°C (425°F), Gas Mark 7, for 5 minutes. Spread with the onion mixture in an even layer. Drain the can of anchovies, reserving the oil. Cut the anchovies into thin strips and use them to make a lattice pattern over the dough. Place the olives in the spaces between the anchovies. Drizzle with the anchovy oil and remaining olive oil.

Return the tart to the oven for 10–15 minutes until golden. Serve warm, scattered with extra thyme sprigs.

For pesto & mushroom tart, make the dough as above, roll out and spread with 5 tablespoons pesto. Fry 300 g (10 oz) sliced mushrooms in 3 tablespoons oil. Scatter over the pesto and finish as above.

minted courgette & lemon loaf

Makes **1 large loaf**

Time **3–4 hours**, depending
on machine, plus standing

1 large **courgette**, about
225 g (7½ oz)

2 tablespoons **salt**, plus
½ teaspoon

175 ml (6 fl oz) **water**

75 ml (3 fl oz) **olive oil**

½ teaspoon freshly ground
black pepper

grated rind of 1 **lemon**

2 tablespoons chopped **mint**

3 tablespoons **capers**, rinsed
and drained

400 g (13 oz) **strong white
bread flour**

1 tablespoon **caster sugar**

1¼ teaspoons **fast-action
dried yeast**

Coarsely grate the courgette and mix in a colander with 2 tablespoons salt. Leave to stand for 30 minutes. Rinse the courgette in plenty of cold water and pat dry between several layers of kitchen paper.

Lift the bread pan out of the machine and fit the blade. Put the ingredients in the pan, following the order specified in the manual.

Fit the pan into the machine and close the lid. Set to a 750 g (1½ lb) loaf size on the basic white programme. Select your preferred crust setting. Add the courgette, lemon, mint and capers when the machine beeps.

At the end of the programme lift the pan out of the machine and shake the bread out on to a wire rack to cool.

For feta & yogurt dip, to serve with the toasted bread, beat 150 ml (5 fl oz) Greek yogurt in a bowl with 150 ml (5 fl oz) mayonnaise. Stir in 2 tablespoons snipped chives and 2 tablespoons chopped parsley. Crumble 100 g (3½ oz) feta into the mixture and mix well. Season with salt and pepper. Turn into a small serving dish, cover and chill until ready to serve.

spinach & manchego ring loaf

Makes **1 large ring loaf**
(about 10 thick slices)

Time **1½–2½ hours**, depending
on machine, plus cooking,
shaping, proving and baking

Dough

2 tablespoons **olive oil**

1 small **onion**, finely chopped

250 ml (8 fl oz) **water**

25 g (1 oz) **Parmesan cheese**,
grated, plus extra for sprinkling

1 teaspoon **salt**

450 g (14½ oz) **strong white
bread flour**

1 tablespoon **caster sugar**

1½ teaspoons **fast-action
dried yeast**

To finish

175 g (6 oz) young **spinach
leaves**

200 g (7 oz) **Manchego
cheese**, cut into small dice

½ teaspoon freshly grated
nutmeg

2 **garlic cloves**, finely chopped

50 g (2 oz) **raisins**

50 g (2 oz) **pine nuts**,
lightly toasted

beaten **egg**, to glaze

salt and **black pepper**

Heat the oil in a frying pan and gently fry the onion
until softened. Leave to cool.

Lift the bread pan out of the machine and fit the blade.
Put the dough ingredients in the pan, following the
order specified in the manual. Add the onion and
cheese with the water. Fit the pan into the machine
and close the lid. Set to the dough programme.

Put the spinach in a saucepan with 1 tablespoon water
and cover with a lid. Heat gently until the spinach has
wilted. Drain and pat the spinach dry between layers of
kitchen paper. In a bowl, mix together the Manchego
with the nutmeg, garlic, raisins, pine nuts and seasoning.

At the end of the programme turn the dough out on to
a floured surface and roll it out to a rectangle, about
40 x 30 cm (15 x 12 inches). Spread the filling almost to
the edges. Roll up the dough, starting from a long side.
Transfer the roll to a large, greased baking sheet with
the join underneath. Bend the ends round to make a
ring and push the ends firmly together to seal. Cover
loosely with oiled clingfilm and leave in a warm place
for about 45 minutes until risen by at least half again.

Brush the dough with beaten egg to glaze and
sprinkle with extra grated Parmesan. Make vertical
scores to the middle of the dough so that the filling is
revealed. Bake in a preheated oven, 200°C (400°F),
Gas Mark 6, for 30–35 minutes until risen and golden.
Serve warm or cold.

For Cheddar cheese & chutney ring, make as above,
filling with 200 g (7 oz) tomato chutney and 250 g
(8 oz) grated Cheddar cheese.

provençal-style picnic slice

Makes **10 thick slices**
Time 1½–2½ **hours**, depending
on machine, plus shaping,
proving and baking

Dough
2 tablespoons **olive oil**
4 tablespoons chopped
   herbs, such as thyme,
   oregano and rosemary
75 g (3 oz) **Parmesan
   cheese**, grated
250 ml (8 fl oz) **milk**
1 teaspoon **salt**
350 g (11½ oz) **strong white
   bread flour**
1 tablespoon **caster sugar**
1 teaspoon **fast-action dried
   yeast**

To finish
5 tablespoons **sun-dried
   tomato paste**
350 g (11½ oz) **mixed roasted
   vegetables**, such as peppers,
   courgettes and red onions
   (see pages 230–31)
2 tablespoons **olive oil**
milk, to brush
25 g (1 oz) **Parmesan cheese**,
   grated, for sprinkling
salt and **black pepper**

Lift the bread pan out of the machine and fit the blade. Put the dough ingredients in the pan, following the order specified in the manual. Add the herbs and cheese with the milk.

Fit the pan into the machine and close the lid. Set to the dough programme.

At the end of the programme turn the dough out on to a floured surface and roll it out to a 28 cm (11 inch) square. Spread with the tomato paste and scatter with the roasted vegetables. Drizzle with the oil and a little salt and pepper.

Roll up the dough so the filling is enclosed and cut it into 10 thick slices. Arrange the slices in a staggered line on a large, greased baking sheet, resting each slice against the one behind so the filling is revealed. Cover with oiled clingfilm and leave to rise in a warm place for about 40 minutes or until almost doubled in size.

Brush the dough with milk and sprinkle with cheese. Bake in a preheated oven, 200°C (400°F), Gas Mark 6, for 25 minutes until risen and golden. Serve warm, broken into slices.

For leek & Stilton picnic loaf, make the dough as above but reducing the Parmesan to 40 g (1½ oz). Thinly slice 350 g (11½ oz) leeks and sauté them in 25 g (1 oz) butter until soft. Leave to cool. Roll out the dough as above and scatter with the leeks, 150 g (5 oz) crumbled, creamy Stilton cheese and plenty of black pepper. Roll up the dough and finish as above.

pancetta & artichoke pizza

Serves **4**

Time **1½–2½ hours**, depending on machine, plus shaping, proving and baking

Dough

200 ml (7 fl oz) **water**

2 tablespoons **olive oil**

1 teaspoon **salt**

300 g (10 oz) **strong white bread flour**

1 teaspoon **caster sugar**

1 teaspoon **fast-action dried yeast**

To finish

275 g (9 oz) jar **artichokes** in olive oil

100 g (3½ oz) sliced **pancetta**, cut into large pieces

5 tablespoons **pesto**

4 tablespoons **pine nuts**

75 g (3 oz) piece **Pecorino cheese** or **Parmesan cheese**, to serve

black pepper

Lift the bread pan out of the machine and fit the blade. Put the dough ingredients in the pan, following the order specified in the manual.

Fit the pan into the machine and close the lid. Set to the dough programme.

Drain the artichokes, reserving 2 tablespoons of the oil, and slice them into smaller pieces. Heat the reserved oil in a frying pan and fry the pancetta until it just starts to colour.

At the end of the programme turn the dough out on to a floured surface and roll it out to a circle 30 cm (12 inches) across. Transfer to a large, greased baking sheet and spread to 1 cm (½ inch) of the edges with the pesto. Scatter with the artichokes, then the pancetta, pine nuts and plenty of black pepper.

Bake in a preheated oven, 200°C (400°F), Gas Mark 6, for about 15 minutes until the crust is pale golden. Shave plenty of cheese over the top to serve.

For goats' cheese & onion pizzas, fry 500 g (1 lb) sliced red onions in 3 tablespoons olive oil until softened. Make the dough as above and cut it into quarters. Roll out each piece to a circle 20 cm (8 inches) across and transfer to 2 greased baking sheets. Scatter with the onions. Thinly slice 200 g (7 oz) goats' cheese and arrange over the top. Scatter each pizza with a few black olives and a sprinkling of chopped oregano. Season with salt and pepper and drizzle each with a teaspoon of olive oil. Bake as above.

potato & thyme bread

Makes **2 small loaves**

Time 1½–2½ **hours**, depending
on machine, plus cooking,
shaping, proving and baking

500 g (1 lb) well-flavoured
floury potatoes, such as
Maris Piper, cut into 1 cm
(½ inch) dice
200 ml (7 fl oz) **milk**
75 g (3 oz) **unsalted butter**,
softened
2 teaspoons **sea salt**, plus
extra for sprinkling
2 tablespoons chopped
lemon thyme
¼ teaspoon **ground turmeric**
475 g (15 oz) **strong white
bread flour**
2 teaspoons **caster sugar**
1½ teaspoons **fast-action
dried yeast**
thyme sprigs, to garnish

Cook the potatoes in boiling, salted water for
10 minutes or until tender. Drain thoroughly and return
150 g (5 oz) to the pan. Mash until smooth; let cool.

Lift the bread pan out of the machine and fit the blade.
Put the ingredients, except the thyme springs, in the
pan, following the order specified in the manual. Add
the mashed potatoes with the milk. Fit the pan into the
machine and close the lid. Set to the dough programme.
Melt the remaining butter.

At the end of the programme, knead in the remaining
diced potatoes. Divide the dough in half and shape into
2 long, slender loaves. Space slightly apart on a large,
greased baking sheet. Cover loosely with oiled clingfilm
and leave to rise in a warm place for 45 minutes.

Brush the loaves with half the melted butter and
sprinkle with sea salt. Bake in a preheated oven, 220°C
(425°F), Gas Mark 7, for 25 minutes until risen and
golden. Brush with the remaining melted butter and
sprinkle with extra thyme leaves. Serve warm or cool.

For spicy potato bread, boil and mash 200 g (7 oz)
potatoes and let cool. Chop 100 g (3½ oz) streaky
bacon and fry in a dash of oil. Put 200 ml (7 fl oz)
milk, 1 teaspoon salt, 2 tablespoons curry paste, 25 g
(1 oz) soft butter, 15 g (½ oz) chopped coriander,
475 g (15 oz) strong white bread flour, 2 teaspoons
caster sugar and 1½ teaspoons fast-action dried yeast
in the bread pan following the order specified in the
manual. Add the potatoes with the milk. Set to a 750 g
(1½ lb) loaf size on the basic white programme. Add
the bacon when the machine beeps.

sweet potato & tarragon bread

Makes **1 large loaf**

Time **3–4 hours**, depending
on machine, plus cooking

200 g (7 oz) **sweet potatoes**

175 ml (6 fl oz) **milk**

50 g (2 oz) **unsalted butter**,
softened

2 teaspoons **salt**

2 teaspoons **Dijon mustard**

4 tablespoons **mustard seeds**

300 g (10 oz) **strong white
bread flour**

175 g (6 oz) **strong wholemeal flour** or **granary flour**

1 teaspoon **caster sugar**

1¼ teaspoons **fast-action
dried yeast**

100 g (3½ oz) firm **goats'
cheese**, diced

5 g (¼ oz) **tarragon**, leaves
pulled from stalks

Peel and dice the sweet potatoes and cook them in
boiling water for about 10 minutes until just tender.
Drain thoroughly, return to the saucepan and mash
until smooth. Leave to cool.

Lift the bread pan out of the machine and fit the blade.
Put the ingredients, except the cheese and tarragon, in
the pan, following the order specified in the manual.
Add the mashed potatoes with the milk.

Fit the pan into the machine and close the lid. Set to
a 750 g (1½ lb) loaf size on the basic white programme.
Select your preferred crust setting. Add the cheese and
tarragon when the machine beeps.

At the end of the programme lift the pan out of the
machine and shake the bread out on to a wire rack
to cool.

For seeded pumpkin bread with cajun spices, peel,
deseed and dice 200 g (7 oz) pumpkin and cook in
boiling water until only just tender. Drain thoroughly
and mash. Put 175 ml (6 fl oz) milk, 50 g (2 oz) soft
butter, 2 teaspoons salt, 2 tablespoons Cajun spice
blend, 475 g (15 oz) strong white bread flour,
1 teaspoon sugar and 1½ teaspoons fast-action dried
yeast in the bread pan, following the order specified
in the manual. (Add the pumpkin mash with the milk
and spice blend with the flour.) Add 5 tablespoons
pumpkin seeds when the machine beeps. After baking
shake the bread out on to a wire rack to cool.

onion & red leicester bread

Makes **1 large loaf**

Time **3–4 hours**, depending
   on machine

1 tablespoon **olive oil**

1 **red onion**, thinly sliced

3 teaspoons **caster sugar**

250 ml (8 fl oz) **water**

100 g (3½ oz) **red Leicester
   cheese**, grated

1 teaspoon **salt**

1 teaspoon **ready-made** or
   powdered English mustard

½ teaspoon **peppercorns**,
   roughly crushed

425 g (14 oz) **strong white
   bread flour**

1¼ teaspoons **fast-action
   dried yeast**

Lift the bread pan out of the machine and fit the blade.
Put the ingredients, except the olive oil, onion and sugar,
in the pan, following the order specified in the manual.

Fit the pan into the machine and close the lid. Set to
a 750 g (1½ lb) loaf size on the basic white programme
with a pale crust setting. (If your machine does not
have a setting for crust colour, set the machine to sweet
bread to prevent the cheese over-darkening the crust).

Heat the oil in a frying pan while the programme is
running. Add the onion and fry over a medium heat for
5 minutes until softened. Sprinkle with 1 teaspoon of
the sugar and fry for 5 more minutes until the onion is
lightly caramelized. Leave to cool.

Add the onions gradually when the machine beeps.

At the end of the programme lift the pan out of the
machine and shake the bread on to a wire rack to cool.

For Stilton & spinach whirl, put 275 ml (9 fl oz) milk,
25 g (1 oz) soft butter, 1 teaspoon salt, 1 teaspoon
ground mace, 425 g (14 oz) strong white bread flour,
1 teaspoon sugar, 1¼ teaspoons fast action dried yeast
in the bread pan, following the order specified in the
manual. Set to the dough programme. Lightly wilt
100 g (3½ oz) washed spinach leaves in a pan. Cool.
Roll out the dough to a 25 cm (10 inch) square and
scatter with the spinach and 200 g (7 oz) crumbled
Stilton. Roll up and drop into a 1.5 kg (3 lb) greased
loaf tin. Cover with oiled clingfilm and leave to rise for
45 minutes. Bake in a preheated oven, 200°C (400°F),
Gas Mark 6, for 35–40 minutes until risen.

pesto & marinated olive bread

Makes **1 large loaf**

Time **3–4 hours**, depending
   on machine

200 ml (7 fl oz) **water**

2 tablespoons **olive oil**

2 tablespoons **pesto**

1 teaspoon **salt**

425 g (14 oz) **strong white
   bread flour**

1 teaspoon **caster sugar**

1¼ teaspoons **fast-action
   dried yeast**

125 g (4 oz) pitted and
   marinated mixed olives,
   halved

Lift the bread pan out of the machine and fit the blade.
Put the ingredients, except the olives, in the pan,
following the order specified in the manual.

Fit the pan into the machine and close the lid. Set to a
750 g (½ lb) loaf size on the basic white programme.
Select your preferred crust setting.

Add the olives when the machine beeps, adding them
gradually to prevent the blade jamming.

At the end of the programme lift the pan out of the
machine and shake the bread out on to a wire rack
to cool.

For Emmenthal & hot pepper bread, use 50 g
(2 oz) hot red Jalapeño chilli peppers from a jar. Pat
dry on kitchen paper and roughly chop. Make the
bread as above, omitting the pesto and olives and
adding the chopped chilli peppers, 100 g (3½ oz)
diced Emmenthal cheese and 15 g (½ oz) chopped
parsley or coriander when the machine beeps.

flat breads

pitta bread

Makes **8 breads**

Time **1½–2½ hours**,
depending on machine, plus
shaping, proving and baking

250 ml (8 fl oz) **water**
1 tablespoon **olive oil**
1 teaspoon **salt**
½ teaspoon **ground cumin**
375 g (12 oz) **strong white
bread flour**
1 teaspoon **caster sugar**
1 teaspoon **fast-action dried
yeast**

Lift the bread pan out of the machine and fit the blade.
Put the ingredients in the pan, following the order
specified in the manual.

Fit the pan into the machine and close the lid. Set to
the dough programme.

At the end of the programme turn the dough out on to
a floured surface and cut it into 8 equal-sized pieces.
Roll out each piece to an oval about 15 cm (6 inches)
long. Arrange in a single layer on a well-floured clean,
dry tea towel. Cover loosely with a second clean, dry tea
towel and leave to rise in a warm place for 30 minutes.

Put a floured baking sheet in a preheated oven,
230°C (450°F), Gas Mark 8, and leave to heat up for
5 minutes. Transfer half the breads to the baking sheet
and cook for 5–6 minutes until just beginning to
colour. Remove from the oven and leave to cool on a
wire rack while you cook the remainder. Wrap the still
warm pittas in a clean, dry tea towel to keep them soft
until ready to serve. If they are left to go cold, warm the
pittas through in a hot oven before serving.

For olive & herb mini pittas, make the dough as
above, but add 50 g (2 oz) pitted and chopped black
olives and a large handful of chopped parsley and
mint to the dough when the machine beeps. At the
end of the programme turn the dough out on to a
floured surface and cut it into 16 pieces. Thinly roll out
each piece to an oval 10–12 cm (4–5 inches) long.
Prove and bake as above.

tomato focaccia

Makes **2 loaves**

Time **1½–2½ hours**,
depending on machine, plus
shaping, proving and baking

Dough

475 g (15 oz) **strong white
bread flour**

1 teaspoon **caster sugar**

1 teaspoon **salt**

1½ teaspoons **fast-action
dried yeast**

3 tablespoons **olive oil**

275 ml (9 fl oz) **water**

To finish

200 g (7 oz) **cherry tomatoes**

a few **rosemary sprigs**

a few **black olives**

1 teaspoon **salt flakes**

3 tablespoons **olive oil**

Lift the bread pan out of the machine and fit the blade.
Put the dough ingredients in the pan, following the
order specified in the manual.

Fit the pan into the machine and close the lid. Set to
the dough programme.

At the end of the programme turn the dough out on to
a floured surface and cut it in half. Press each into a
rough oval a little larger than your hand.

Transfer the loaves to 2 greased baking sheets and
use the end of a wooden spoon to make indentations
over the surface. Press the tomatoes into some of the
indentations, add small sprigs of rosemary and olives
into some of the others. Sprinkle with salt flakes and
leave, uncovered, for 20 minutes.

Drizzle the loaves with a little of the oil and bake in a
preheated oven, 200°C (400°F), Gas Mark 6, for
15 minutes. Swap the shelf positions during cooking
so that both loaves brown evenly. Drizzle with the
remaining oil and serve warm or cold, torn into pieces.

For onion, sage & gorgonzola focaccia, make the
dough as above, adding 1 tablespoon chopped sage
with the flour. After shaping and making indentations,
scatter the loaves with ½ small red onion, very finely
sliced, and 75 g (3 oz) crumbled Gorgonzola. Drizzle
with olive oil as above and scatter with small sage
leaves halfway through baking.

semolina & olive oil bread

Makes **6 breads**

Time **1½–2½ hours**,
depending on machine, plus
shaping, proving and baking

175 ml (6 fl oz) **water**

100 ml (3½ fl oz) **olive oil**

2 teaspoons **salt**

200 g (7 oz) **strong white
bread flour**

200 g (7 oz) fine **semolina**,
plus extra for sprinkling

1 teaspoon **fast-action dried
yeast**

Lift the bread pan out of the machine and fit the blade.
Put the ingredients in the pan, following the order
specified in the manual.

Fit the pan into the machine and close the lid. Set to
the dough programme.

At the end of the programme turn the dough out on to
a floured surface and divide it into 6 equal pieces.
Shape each into a ball and roll it out until about 15 cm
(6 inches) in diameter.

Grease a large baking sheet and dust it with semolina.
Space the breads about 2 cm (¾ inch) apart on the
baking sheet and sprinkle with extra semolina. Press
the semolina down gently. Cover loosely with oiled
clingfilm and leave to rise in a warm place for
30 minutes.

Bake in a preheated oven, 220°C (425°F), Gas Mark 7,
for 12–15 minutes until golden. Transfer to a wire rack
to cool.

For chorizo & broad bean tostadas, make the bread
as above and cool. Cut 300 g (10 oz) piece chorizo
sausage into 1 cm (½ inch) dice. Cook 200 g (7 oz)
baby broad beans in boiling water for 3 minutes. Drain
and cool, then pop the beans out of their skins into a
bowl. Heat 4 tablespoons extra-virgin olive oil in a
frying pan and gently fry the chorizo and 2 thinly sliced
shallots for 5 minutes, stirring. Toss with the beans,
2 teaspoons lemon juice and a little salt and pepper.
Place each bread under a medium grill until toasted.
Serve topped with the warm or cold chorizo and
broad bean mix.

piadina

Makes **8 breads**

Time **1½–2½ hours**,
depending on machine, plus
shaping, proving and baking

300 ml (½ pint) **water**

25 g (1 oz) **lard**, melted

2 teaspoons **salt**

2 teaspoons **fennel seeds**,
crushed

450 g (14½ oz) **strong white
bread flour**

1 teaspoon **caster sugar**

1¼ teaspoons **fast-action
dried yeast**

Lift the bread pan out of the machine and fit the blade. Put the ingredients in the pan, following the order specified in the manual.

Fit the pan into the machine and close the lid. Set to the dough programme.

At the end of the programme turn the dough out on to a floured surface and divide it into 8 equal pieces. Roll out each piece to a circle 23 cm (9 inches) across. Leave the rounds on the floured surface, covered with a clean, dry tea towel for 15 minutes.

Heat a large frying pan or griddle until very hot then reduce to the lowest setting. Place a piece of dough in the pan and cook for 5–6 minutes until golden brown. Pierce any large bubbles that form with a fork and turn the bread several times so that it doesn't start to catch.

Slide the piadina on to a tray or plate and keep covered with a clean, damp tea towel to keep the bread soft and warm while you cook the remainder.

For Italian wraps with mozzarella & cured meats, spread a hot piadina with 1–2 teaspoons pesto. Thinly slice 75 g (3 oz) mozzarella cheese and scatter on top. Drizzle with a little extra-virgin olive oil and plenty of black pepper. Arrange slices of cured meat (such as prosciutto, coppa or salami) over the cheese. Scatter with rocket leaves, if liked. Fold the piadina into 3 to serve.

buttered garlic & basil sticks

Makes **about 20 sticks**

Time **1½–2½ hours**,
   depending on machine, plus
   shaping, proving and baking

Dough

200 ml (7 fl oz) **water**

2 tablespoons **olive oil**

1 teaspoon **salt**

400 g (13 oz) **strong white
   bread flour**

1 teaspoon **caster sugar**

1¼ teaspoons **fast-action
   dried yeast**

To finish

100 g (3½ oz) **unsalted butter**

4 **garlic cloves**, finely
   chopped

small bunch of **basil**, leaves
   torn into pieces

coarse sea salt

black pepper

Lift the bread pan out of the machine and fit the blade. Put the dough ingredients in the pan, following the order specified in the manual. Fit the pan into the machine and close the lid. Set to the dough programme.

At the end of the programme turn the dough out on to a floured surface and cut it in half. Roll each half to a thin oval about 35 x 18 cm (14 x 7 inches). Transfer to 2 greased baking sheets and cut into 2.5 cm (1 inch) strips, making cuts a little in from the edge of the dough so the strips are still held together at the ends.

Sprinkle the dough with a little coarse salt. Cover loosely with oiled clingfilm and leave in a warm place for 30 minutes or until the dough has risen around the edges.

Bake in a preheated oven, 220°C (425°F), Gas Mark 7, for 8–10 minutes until the bread sounds hollow when tapped with the fingertips. Transfer to 2 large plates.

Melt a small piece of butter in a saucepan and fry the garlic for 2–3 minutes until beginning to brown. Add the remaining butter, the basil leaves and pepper to taste. When the butter has melted, brush this over the hot bread, separate into sticks and serve immediately.

For cumin & coriander sticks, make the dough as above, adding 2 teaspoons crushed cumin seeds. Melt 25 g (1 oz) butter in a saucepan and gently fry 1 finely chopped spring onion and 1 thinly sliced red chilli. Add 4 tablespoons chopped coriander and 75 g (3 oz) more butter. Heat until the butter has melted, then brush it over the hot bread.

turkish pide

Makes **4 pide**
Time **1½–2½ hours**,
    depending on machine, plus
    shaping, proving and baking

Dough
125 ml (4 fl oz) **water**
125 ml (4 fl oz) **natural yogurt**
2 tablespoons **olive oil**
2 teaspoons **salt**
4 tablespoons **sesame seeds**
400 g (13 oz) **strong white
    bread flour**
1 teaspoon **caster sugar**
1 teaspoon **fast-action dried
    yeast**

To finish
4 tablespoons **olive oil**
1 large **onion**, chopped
2 **garlic cloves**, chopped
250 g (8 oz) **minced lamb**
good pinch of **saffron strands**
1 tablespoon **coriander
    seeds**, lightly crushed
75 g (3 oz) ready-to-eat **dried
    apricots**, sliced
65 g (2½ oz) **pine nuts**
salt and **black pepper**
chopped **parsley**, for sprinkling

Lift the bread pan out of the machine and fit the blade. Put the dough ingredients in the pan, following the order specified in the manual. Add the sesame seeds with the flour.

Fit the pan into the machine and close the lid. Set to the dough programme.

Make the topping. Heat 2 tablespoons oil in a frying pan and fry the onion for 5 minutes to soften. Add the garlic and lamb and fry for 5–10 minutes until beginning to brown, breaking up the lamb with a wooden spoon. Stir in the saffron, coriander, apricots and pine nuts and cook, stirring, for 5 minutes. Season with salt and pepper.

At the end of the programme turn the dough out on to a floured surface and cut it into quarters. Roll each piece to an oval, about 20 cm (8 inches) long. Transfer to 2 greased baking sheets and prick the bases with a fork. Scatter with the meat mixture to about 1 cm (½ inch) of the edges. Cover loosely with oiled clingfilm and leave to rise in a warm place for 30 minutes.

Drizzle the remaining oil over the breads and bake in a preheated oven, 200°C (400°F), Gas Mark 6, for about 20 minutes until golden. Serve sprinkled with parsley.

For feta & onion pide, make and shape the dough as above. Transfer to the baking sheets and prick with a fork. Scatter 200 g (7 oz) crumbled feta cheese over the dough to 1 cm (½ inch) of the edges. Chop 4 spring onions and lightly crush 1 teaspoon cumin seeds. Scatter the onions and seeds over the feta and season with salt and pepper. Leave to rise as above and drizzle each pide with 1 tablespoon olive oil before cooking.

fougasse

Makes **2 loaves**

Time **1½–2½ hours**,
  depending on machine, plus
  shaping, proving and baking

250 ml (8 fl oz) **water**

4 tablespoons **olive oil**, plus
  extra for drizzling

1½ teaspoons **salt**

3 tablespoons fresh chopped
  or 1½ teaspoons dried
  mixed herbs, such as
  lavender, thyme and
  rosemary

475 g (15 oz) **strong white
  bread flour**

2 teaspoons **caster sugar**

1¼ teaspoons **fast-action
  dried yeast**

coarse sea salt, for sprinkling

Lift the bread pan out of the machine and fit the blade. Add the ingredients to the pan, following the order specified in the manual.

Fit the pan into the machine and close the lid. Set to the dough programme.

At the end of the programme turn the dough out on to a floured surface and cut it in half. Roll each half to an oval 30 x 20 cm (12 x 8 inches).

Transfer the dough to 2 greased baking sheets. Make 5 diagonal slits in the dough, then open out the outer edges of the slits by lifting the edges of the bread and widening the gap with a fingertip. Cover loosely with oiled clingfilm and leave in a warm place to rise for 30 minutes or until puffy.

Bake in a preheated oven, 220°C (425°F), Gas Mark 7, for 8–10 minutes until golden. Drizzle with a little olive oil and scatter over a little sea salt. Transfer to a wire rack after 10 minutes to cool completely.

For Parmesan & olive bread sticks, make the dough as above, adding 50 g (2 oz) finely chopped black olives and 50 g (2 oz) grated Parmesan cheese when the machine beeps. Roll out the dough on a floured surface to a rectangle, about 30 x 20 cm (12 x 8 inches). Cover loosely with a floured, clean tea towel and leave to stand for 20 minutes. Cut across into long, thin strips and space, slightly apart, on a greased and semolina-dusted baking sheet. Brush lightly with beaten egg and sprinkle with salt. Bake in a preheated oven, 220°C (425°F), Gas Mark 7, for 15–20 minutes until golden. Cool on a wire rack.

seeded naan breads

Makes **6 breads**
Time **1½–2½ hours**,
   depending on machine,
   plus shaping, proving
   and cooking

12 **cardamom pods**
2 teaspoons **coriander seeds**
2 teaspoons **cumin seeds**
100 ml (3½ fl oz) **water**
4 tablespoons **natural yogurt**
1 tablespoon **vegetable oil**
1 teaspoon **salt**
2 teaspoons **black onion
   seeds**
275 g (9 oz) **strong white
   bread flour**
1 teaspoon **caster sugar**
¾ teaspoon **fast-action dried
   yeast**
25 g (1 oz) **butter** or **ghee**,
   melted

Crush the cardamom pods using a pestle and mortar to release the seeds. Discard the shells. Add the coriander and cumin seeds and grind until crushed.

Lift the bread pan out of the machine and fit the blade. Put the ingredients, except the butter or ghee, in the pan, following the order specified in the manual. Add all the seeds with the flour. Fit the pan into the machine and close the lid. Set to the dough programme.

At the end of the programme turn the dough out on to a floured surface and divide it into 6 pieces. Roll each out to a tear shape about 22 cm (8½ inches) long. Place on floured trays; dust with flour. Cover loosely with a clean, dry tea towel; leave to rise in a warm place for 20 minutes.

Preheat the grill to its highest setting and heat a large baking sheet under the grill. Brush the dough with the butter or ghee and cook on the baking sheet in 2 or 3 batches until puffy and patchily brown. Stack the cooked breads on a plate and cover with a clean, dry tea towel while you cook the remainder.

For Peshwari naan, omit the seeds. Mix together 50 g (2 oz) ground almonds, 25 g (1 oz) desiccated coconut, 25 g (1 oz) sultanas and a pinch of sugar. Divide the dough into 12 pieces and roll each out to a tear shape, about 12 cm (5 inches) long. Dampen the edges of half the shapes with water and scatter the nut mixture in the centre. Drizzle with 25 g (1 oz) melted butter. Place the remaining pieces of dough on top and re-roll so that the breads are about 22 cm (8½ inches) long. Brush with butter or ghee and cook as above.

asian-style flatbreads

Makes **8 breads**
Time **1½–2½ hours**,
 depending on machine,
 plus shaping, proving
 and cooking

50 g (2 oz) **sesame seeds**
225 ml (7½ fl oz) **water**
1 **garlic clove**, chopped
25 g (1 oz) **fresh root ginger**, grated
25 g (1 oz) roughly chopped **fresh coriander**
2 tablespoons **sesame oil**
2 teaspoons **salt**
450 g (14½ oz) **strong white bread flour**
1 tablespoon **caster sugar**
1¼ teaspoons **fast-action dried yeast**

Put the sesame seeds in a food processor and grind until broken up. (The seeds won't grind to a powder.)

Lift the bread pan out of the machine and fit the blade. Put the ingredients in the pan, following the order specified in the manual. Add the seeds, garlic, ginger and coriander with the water.

Fit the pan into the machine and close the lid. Set to the dough programme.

At the end of the programme turn the dough out on to a floured surface and divide it into 8 equal pieces. Roll out each piece to a circle 20 cm (8 inches) across. Leave the rounds on the floured surface, covered with a clean, dry tea towel, for 15 minutes.

Heat a large frying pan or griddle, then reduce to the lowest setting. Place a piece of dough in the pan and cook for 3–4 minutes, turning once, until golden brown in places. Slide the bread on to a plate and cover with a clean, damp tea towel while you cook the rest.

For spicy chicken wraps, diagonally slice 1 bunch of spring onions. Thinly slice 2 celery sticks. Heat 3 tablespoons vegetable oil in a large frying pan and fry the onions and celery for 2 minutes. Drain to a plate. Add 3 thinly sliced chicken breast fillets to the pan and fry quickly, stirring, for about 5 minutes or until cooked through. Add 4 tablespoons sweet chilli sauce and 2 teaspoons rice wine vinegar. Return the onions and celery to the pan and stir to mix. Spoon the filling across 4 of the wraps (the remainder can be chilled or frozen for another time) and scatter with pea shoots or sprouting beans. Roll up and serve warm.

spiced chickpea flatbreads

Makes **12 breads**

Time **1½–2½ hours**,
   depending on machine, plus
   shaping, proving and baking

100 g (3½ oz) **tahini paste**

2 tablespoons **olive oil**

2 teaspoons **salt**

1 tablespoon **baharat spice
   blend** (see below)

375 g (12 oz) **kamut bread
   flour**

2 tablespoons **light
   muscovado sugar**

1 teaspoon **fast-action dried
   yeast**

Put the tahini paste in a measuring jug and make it up to 275 ml (9 fl oz) with hot water. Stir until the tahini paste has softened, then leave until only just warm.

Lift the bread pan out of the machine and fit the blade. Put the ingredients in the pan, following the order specified in the manual. Add the spice with the flour.

Fit the pan into the machine and close the lid. Set to the dough programme.

At the end of the programme turn the dough out on to a floured surface and divide it into 12 equal pieces. Roll out each piece to an oval about 12 cm (5 inches) long. Arrange them in a single layer on a well-floured, clean, dry tea towel. Cover loosely with a second, clean tea towel and leave to rise in a warm place for 20 minutes.

Put 2 floured baking sheets in a preheated oven, 230°C (450°F), Gas Mark 8, and leave to heat up for 5 minutes. Transfer the breads to the baking sheets and cook for 5–6 minutes until they are just beginning to colour. Remove them from the oven and wrap in a clean, dry tea towel to keep them soft until you are ready to serve.

For homemade baharat spice blend, put 1 teaspoon each of black peppercorns, coriander seeds, cumin seeds and whole cloves in a small, dry frying pan. Add the seeds from 10 cardamom pods and half a crumbled cinnamon stick and dry-fry the spices until they are lightly toasted. Cool slightly and tip into a spice mill or coffee grinder reserved for grinding spices, and blend until finely ground. Tip into a bowl and stir in 1 teaspoon ground paprika and ½ teaspoon freshly ground nutmeg. Store in an airtight container for up to 1 month.

individual
breads

cinnamon doughnuts

Makes **10 doughnuts**
Time **1½–2½ hours**, depending
    on machine, plus shaping,
    proving and cooking

Dough
1 large **egg**, beaten
225 ml (7½ fl oz) **milk**
2 teaspoons **vanilla extract**
25 g (1 oz) **unsalted butter**,
    softened
½ teaspoon **salt**
450 g (14½ oz) **strong white
    bread flour**
50 g (2 oz) **caster sugar**
1¼ teaspoons **fast-action
    dried yeast**

To finish
100 g (3½ oz) **caster sugar**
1 teaspoon **ground cinnamon**
oil, for deep frying

Lift the bread pan out of the machine and fit the blade. Put the dough ingredients in the pan, following the order specified in the manual.

Fit the pan into the machine and close the lid. Set to the dough programme.

At the end of the programme turn the dough out on to a floured surface and cut it into 10 equal pieces. Shape each into a ball and space them, well apart, on a large, greased baking sheet. Cover loosely with oiled clingfilm and leave to rise in a warm place for 30–40 minutes or until almost doubled in size.

Mix together the sugar and cinnamon on a plate. Put 8 cm (3 inches) oil in a large saucepan and heat it until a small piece of bread sizzles on the surface and turns pale golden in about 30 seconds.

Fry the doughnuts, 3–4 at a time, for about 3 minutes, turning them once until golden on both sides. Drain with a slotted spoon on to several sheets of kitchen paper. Cook the remainder. Roll the doughnuts in the cinnamon sugar while still warm. Serve freshly baked with strawberry jam and whipped cream, if liked.

For doughnuts with chocolate sauce, make the dough and leave to rise as above. Place 100 g (3½ oz) chopped plain chocolate in a heatproof bowl with 15 g (½ oz) butter, 4 tablespoons icing sugar and 2 tablespoons milk. Rest the bowl over a pan of gently simmering water and leave until melted, stirring frequently until smooth. Fry the doughnuts as above, draining them and rolling in the spiced sugar. Serve with little pots of the chocolate sauce.

grissini

Makes **about 32 sticks**
Time **1½–2½ hours**,
  depending on machine,
  plus shaping, proving
  and baking

Dough
275 ml (9 fl oz) **water**
3 tablespoons **olive oil**
1 teaspoon **salt**
475 g (15 oz) **strong white**
  bread flour
1½ teaspoons **caster sugar**
1¼ teaspoons **fast-action**
  dried yeast

To finish
5 teaspoons **sesame seeds**
2 teaspoons **fennel seeds**
1 tablespoon chopped
  rosemary, **basil** or **chives**
1 **egg yolk**, to glaze
1 teaspoon **sea salt flakes**,
  for sprinkling

Lift the bread pan out of the machine and fit the blade. Put the dough ingredients in the pan, following the order specified in the manual.

Fit the pan into the machine and close the lid. Set to the dough programme.

At the end of the programme turn the dough out on to a floured surface and cut it into 4 pieces. Leave one piece plain, knead the sesame seeds into the second piece, the fennel seeds into the third, and the chopped herbs into the last piece. Cut each quarter into 8 pieces, then roll each piece into a rope about 25 cm (10 inches) long. Transfer to 2 greased baking sheets. Cover loosely with oiled clingfilm; leave in a warm place for 30 minutes or until the dough is well risen.

Brush the breadsticks with the egg yolk mixed with 1 tablespoon water. Sprinkle the plain ones with the salt flakes. Bake in a preheated oven, 200°C (400°F), Gas Mark 6, for 6–8 minutes or until golden. Transfer to a wire rack to cool.

For grissini with aromatic salt, crumble half a small bay leaf into a coffee grinder (reserved for grinding herbs and spices) with ½ teaspoon each chopped thyme and rosemary and ¼ teaspoon each celery seeds and crushed dried chillies. Add 1 teaspoon sea salt flakes and grind lightly. (Alternatively pound using a pestle and mortar.) Stir in another 1 teaspoon sea salt. Make the grissini dough as above, then shape without adding the seeds or herbs. Brush with the egg yolk glaze and sprinkle with the aromatic salt. Finish as above.

fruited teacakes

Makes **8 teacakes**

Time **1½–2½ hours**,
depending on machine, plus
shaping, proving and baking

Dough

300 ml (½ pint) **milk**

50 g (2 oz) **unsalted butter**,
softened

½ teaspoon **salt**

1 teaspoon **ground mixed
spice**

2 teaspoons **vanilla bean
paste** or **vanilla extract**

450 g (14½ oz) **strong white
bread flour**

75 g (3 oz) **light muscovado
sugar**

1¼ teaspoons **fast-action
dried yeast**

150 g (5 oz) **mixed dried
fruit**, to glaze

To finish

beaten **egg**, to glaze

caster sugar, for sprinkling

Lift the bread pan out of the machine and fit the blade.
Put the dough ingredients, except the dried fruit, in the
pan, following the order specified in the manual.

Fit the pan into the machine and close the lid. Set to
the dough programme, adding the dried fruit when the
machine beeps.

At the end of the programme turn the dough out on to
a floured surface and cut it into 8 equal pieces. Shape
each piece into a ball and space them, about 3 cm
(1¼ inches) apart, on a large, greased baking sheet.
Cover loosely with oiled clingfilm and leave to rise in
a warm place for about 30 minutes or until almost
doubled in size.

Brush with beaten egg to glaze and bake in a preheated
oven, 220°C (425°F), Gas Mark 7, for 15–20 minutes
until risen and golden. Transfer to a wire rack to
cool and sprinkle with the caster sugar. Serve split
and buttered.

For iced finger buns, beat 2 eggs and make up to
300 ml (½ pint) with milk. Continue to make the dough
as above, omitting the mixed spice and dried fruit, and
using the milk and egg mixture to replace the 300 ml
(½ pint) milk. Turn the dough out on to a floured
surface and cut it into 8 equal pieces. Shape each
into finger roll shapes and arrange them on a greased
baking sheet, spacing them about 4 cm (1½ inches)
apart. Leave the buns to rise and bake as above.
Once cooled, spread the tops with glacé icing, made
by mixing together 100 g (3½ oz) icing sugar with
2–3 teaspoons lemon or orange juice.

salted pretzels

Makes **35–40 pretzels**
Time **1½–2½ hours**,
    depending on machine,
    plus shaping, proving
    and baking

Dough
275 ml (9 fl oz) **milk**
1 teaspoon **salt**
300 g (10 oz) **strong white
    bread flour**
75 g (3 oz) **rye flour**
1 tablespoon **caster sugar**
1 teaspoon **fast-action dried
    yeast**

To finish
4 teaspoons **sea salt**
2 teaspoons **caster sugar**

Lift the bread pan out of the machine and fit the blade. Put the dough ingredients in the pan, following the order specified in the manual. Fit the pan into the machine and close the lid. Set to the dough programme.

Put 2 teaspoons sea salt in a small saucepan with the sugar and 3 tablespoons water. Heat until the salt and sugar dissolve, then turn into a small bowl. Grease 2 baking sheets.

At the end of the programme turn the dough out on to a floured surface and roll it out to a rectangle, about 35 x 25 cm (14 x 10 inches). Cover loosely with a clean, dry tea towel and leave to stand for 20 minutes. Cut the rectangle across at 1 cm (½ inch) intervals. Take a piece of dough and bend the ends around to meet, twisting the ends together. Press the ends down on to the curved side of the rope to shape the pretzel. Use the remaining dough to make more pretzels and place them on 2 large, greased baking sheets. Cover loosely with oiled clingfilm and leave for a further 20 minutes.

Bake in a preheated oven, 220°C (425°F), Gas Mark 7, for 8 minutes until golden. Brush with the salt glaze and sprinkle with more salt. Cool on a wire rack.

For garlic & rosemary twigs, make the dough as above, adding 1 crushed garlic clove and 1 tablespoon finely chopped rosemary with the milk. Roll out the dough and cut into 25 cm (10 inch) strips, then through the centre into shorter sticks. Brush with 1 egg yolk, mixed with 2 teaspoons water and 1 teaspoon sugar. Place on greased baking sheets, sprinkle with salt and bake as above.

chorizo & manchego buns

Makes **12 buns**

Time **1½–2½ hours**,
   depending on machine, plus
   shaping, proving and baking

225 ml (7½ fl oz) **water**

3 tablespoons **olive oil**

100 g (3½ oz) **Manchego
cheese**, grated

1 teaspoon **salt**

1 teaspoon ground **hot
paprika**

450 g (14½ oz) **strong white
bread flour**

2 teaspoons **caster sugar**

1¼ teaspoons **fast-action
dried yeast**

125 g (4 oz) **chorizo
sausage**, diced

Lift the bread pan out of the machine and fit the blade. Put the ingredients, except the chorizo, in the pan, following the order specified in the manual.

Fit the pan into the machine and close the lid. Set to the dough programme, adding the chorizo when the machine beeps.

At the end of the programme turn the dough out on to a floured surface and divide it into 12 equal pieces. Shape each piece into a ball. Cut 12 x 15 cm (6 inch) squares of baking parchment. Push a parchment square down into the section of a muffin or Yorkshire pudding tray and drop a ball of dough into it. Repeat with the remainder. Cover loosely with a clean, dry tea towel and leave in a warm place for 30 minutes until risen.

Use a pair of kitchen scissors to snip across the top of each bun. Bake in a preheated oven, 220°C (425°F), Gas Mark 7, for 20 minutes until risen and golden. Transfer to a wire rack to cool.

For prosciutto & Parmesan crown, fry 100 g (3½ oz) chopped prosciutto in 1 tablespoon olive oil until lightly browned. Make the dough as above, using 75 g (3 oz) grated Parmesan cheese instead of the Manchego and adding the prosciutto when the machine beeps. Once the dough is shaped into balls, fit them into a greased 20 cm (8 inch) round cake tin. Leave to rise and bake as above, but increasing the cooking time to 25–30 minutes. After baking, transfer to a wire rack to cool and serve, torn into individual buns.

goats' cheese & bean mini loaves

Makes **10 loaves**
Time **1½–2½ hours**,
   depending on machine, plus
   shaping, proving and baking

Dough
275 ml (9 fl oz) **water**
3 tablespoons **olive oil**
3 tablespoons snipped **chives**
½ teaspoon **black pepper**,
   plus extra for sprinkling
1½ teaspoons **salt**
475 g (15 oz) **strong white
   bread flour**
1 teaspoon **caster sugar**
1¼ teaspoons **fast-action
   dried yeast**

To finish
100 g (3½ oz) frozen **baby
   broad beans** or **soya beans**
200 g (7 oz) soft **goats'
   cheese**, diced
milk, to brush

Lift the bread pan out of the machine and fit the blade. Put the dough ingredients in the pan, following the order specified in the manual.

Fit the pan into the machine and close the lid. Set to the dough programme.

Cook the beans in boiling water for 1 minute. Rinse in cold water and pat dry on kitchen paper.

At the end of the programme turn the dough out on to a floured surface, scatter with the beans and cheese and knead them into the dough until evenly distributed. Cut the dough into 10 equal pieces.

Grease 10 individual loaf tins and place them on a baking sheet. Press each piece of dough into a tin. (If you don't have any individual tins, shape the dough into balls and space them slightly apart on the baking sheet.) Cover loosely with oiled clingfilm and leave to rise in a warm place for 30–40 minutes or until almost doubled in size.

Brush with a little milk, sprinkle with extra black pepper and bake in a preheated oven, 220°C (425°F), Gas Mark 7, for 20–25 minutes until risen and pale golden. Transfer to a wire rack to cool.

For feta, mint & cucumber rolls, make the dough as above, adding 2 tablespoons chopped mint when the machine beeps. Knead 200 g (7 oz) crumbled feta cheese and 75 g (3 oz) drained and chopped pickled cucumber into the dough instead of the beans and goats' cheese. Shape into 10 balls and space slightly apart on a greased baking sheet. Finish as above.

mini dinner rolls

Makes **10 rolls**

Time **1½–2½ hours**, depending on machine, plus shaping, proving and baking

Dough

275 ml (9 fl oz) **water**

30 g (1½ oz) **unsalted butter,** softened

1 teaspoon **salt**

475 g (15 oz) **strong white bread flour**

1 teaspoon **caster sugar**

1¼ teaspoons **fast-action dried yeast**

To finish

1 **egg yolk**, to glaze

poppy seeds or **black mustard seeds, sesame seeds, fennel seeds, paprika, rosemary sprigs, coarsely ground Cajun spice** and **coarse sea salt**

Lift the bread pan out of the machine and fit the blade. Put the dough ingredients in the pan, following the order specified in the manual. Fit the pan into the machine and close the lid. Set to the dough programme. At the end of the programme turn the dough out on to a floured surface and cut it into 10 pieces.

Take 2 pieces of dough and shape each into a rope 25 cm (10 inches) long. Roll up each piece to make a spiral. Take 2 pieces of dough and divide each into 3 small balls. Arrange these in a triangle with the balls touching to make clover leaf shapes. Take 2 pieces of dough and shape each into a round. Make 5 or 6 cuts with scissors from the edge to the centre of each one. Take 2 pieces of dough and shape each into a rope 23 cm (9 inches) long. Loop 1 end of 1 rope, then thread the other end through the loop to make a knot. Repeat with the other piece. Take 2 pieces of dough and shape into ovals. Make 4 small cuts across the top of each with scissors and insert sprigs of rosemary into them. Arrange the shapes on large, greased baking sheets.

Cover loosely with oiled clingfilm and leave in a warm place to rise for 20 minutes. Brush with the egg yolk mixed with 1 tablespoon of water and sprinkle with seeds, spices, herbs or salt. Bake in a preheated oven, 200°C (400°F), Gas Mark 6, for 10 minutes until golden. Transfer to a wire rack to cool.

For pesto & olive dinner rolls, make the dough as above, using 2 tablespoons pesto to replace 25 ml (1 fl oz) of the water. Add 50 g (2 oz) chopped black or green olives when the machine beeps. Shape into individual rolls and bake as above.

spicy swirls

Makes **12 spirals**

Time **1½–2½ hours**,
  depending on machine, plus
  shaping, proving and baking

2 teaspoons crushed **dried chillies**

2 teaspoons **cumin seeds**

1 tablespoon **coriander seeds**

2 teaspoons **fennel seeds**

275 ml (9 fl oz) **water**

2 tablespoons **sunflower oil**

1 teaspoon **salt**

475 g (15 oz) **strong white bread flour**

1 teaspoon **caster sugar**

1¼ teaspoons **fast-action dried yeast**

1 **egg yolk**, to glaze

Crush the dried chillies, cumin, coriander and fennel seeds using a pestle and mortar. Reserve 1 teaspoon for sprinkling. Lift the bread pan out of the machine and fit the blade. Put the ingredients in the pan, following the order specified in the manual. Add the crushed spices with the flour.

Fit the pan into the machine and close the lid. Set to the dough programme.

At the end of the programme turn the dough out on to a floured surface and cut it into 12 equal pieces. Roll each piece into a rope about 30 cm (12 inches) long. Roll each rope into a spiral shape and place on 2 large, greased baking sheets, spacing them well apart. Cover loosely with oiled clingfilm and leave to rise in a warm place for 25–30 minutes or until almost doubled in size.

Mix the egg yolk with 1 teaspoon water and brush over the dough. Sprinkle with the reserved crushed spices, following the pattern of the spirals.

Bake in a preheated oven, 220°C (425°F), Gas Mark 7, for 8–10 minutes until golden and the bases sound hollow when tapped. Transfer to a wire rack to cool.

For sesame knots, put 50 g (2 oz) sesame seeds in a small, dry frying pan and heat gently, shaking the pan frequently, until the seeds start to toast. Make the dough as above, using the toasted seeds instead of the crushed spices. Divide the dough into 12 equal pieces and shape each into a rope, about 23 cm (9 inches) long. Tie each into a knot shape and space well apart on the baking sheets. Finish as above, sprinkling the knots with sesame seeds.

mini parsnip loaves

Makes **10 loaves**
Time **1½–2½ hours**,
   depending on machine, plus
   cooking, shaping, proving
   and baking

150 g (5 oz) small **parsnips**,
   cut into chunks
2 tablespoons **olive oil**
large pinch of **saffron**
   threads, crumbled
1½ teaspoons **salt**
450 g (14½ oz) **strong white**
   bread flour
1 teaspoon **caster sugar**
1¼ teaspoons **fast-action**
   dried yeast
4 tablespoons chopped
   parsley
1 medium strength **red chilli**,
   deseeded and thinly sliced
milk, to brush

Cook the parsnips in boiling water for 10 minutes until just tender. Drain, reserving the liquid, and mash the parsnips. Leave to cool.

Measure 275 ml (9 fl oz) of the cooking juices, making up the quantity with water if necessary. Lift the bread pan out of the machine and fit the blade. Put the ingredients, except the parsley and chilli, in the pan, following the order specified in the manual. Add the mashed parsnips with the liquid. Fit the pan into the machine and close the lid. Set to the dough programme, adding the parsley and chilli when the machine beeps.

At the end of the programme turn the dough out on to a floured surface and cut it into 10 equal pieces. Grease 10 x 150 ml (¼ pint) dariole moulds. Shape each piece of dough into a ball and drop into the prepared tins. Place on a baking sheet and cover loosely with oiled clingfilm. Leave in a warm place for 25–30 minutes or until the dough has just risen above the tops of the tins.

Brush with milk and bake in a preheated oven, 220°C (425°F), Gas Mark 7, for 10–15 minutes until golden and the bases of the bread sound hollow when tapped with the fingertips. Transfer to a wire rack to cool.

For wholemeal carrot & onion loaves, cook 150 g (5 oz) carrots in plenty of water until just tender. Drain and mash, reserving 275 ml (9 fl oz) of the cooking liquid. Fry 1 small chopped onion in 1 tablespoon olive oil until tender. Continue to make the bread as above using the carrots and liquid to replace the parsnips and replacing 200 g (7 oz) of the white flour with wholemeal flour.

cherry tomato & basil buns

Makes **8 buns**

Time **1½–2½ hours**,
    depending on machine, plus
    shaping, proving and baking

Dough

300 ml (½ pint) **water**

25 g (1 oz) **basil leaves**

6 tablespoons extra-virgin
    olive oil

1½ teaspoons **salt**

½ teaspoon **dried oregano**

475 g (15 oz) **strong white
    bread flour**

1 teaspoon **caster sugar**

1¼ teaspoons **fast-action
    dried yeast**

2 tablespoons **capers**,
    rinsed and drained

To finish

4 tablespoons **sun-dried
    tomato paste**

600 g (1 lb 2 oz) **cherry
    tomatoes**, halved

150 ml (5 fl oz) **Greek yogurt**

4 tablespoons **mayonnaise**

½ teaspoon **black pepper**

salt

Tear half the basil leaves into small pieces. Lift the bread pan out of the machine and fit the blade. Add the water, 3 tablespoons olive oil, salt, oregano, flour, sugar and yeast to the pan, following the order specified in the manual.

Fit the pan into the machine and close the lid. Set to the dough programme, adding the torn basil leaves and capers when the machine beeps.

At the end of the programme turn the dough out on to a floured surface and divide it into 8 equal pieces. Roll each piece roughly into a round shape, about 15 cm (6 inches) across, and space them, about 5 cm (2 inches) apart, on 2 large, greased baking sheets. Cover with oiled clingfilm and leave to rise in a warm place for 30 minutes.

Dot with the tomato paste to about 1 cm (½ inch) of the edges. Pile the tomato halves on top. Bake in a preheated oven, 230°C (450°F), Gas Mark 8, for about 15 minutes until risen and the tomatoes are soft.

Meanwhile, chop the remaining basil and mix with the yogurt, mayonnaise, pepper and a little salt. Transfer the buns to serving plates and drizzle with the remaining oil and a little more salt. Serve with the yogurt on the side.

For asparagus & tarragon buns, make the dough as above, adding a handful of tarragon leaves to the dough instead of the basil. Trim 400 g (13 oz) fine asparagus tips, cutting them in half if long, and blanch in boiling water for 1 minute. Divide the dough as above and roll it out to ovals, each about 18 cm (7 inches) long. After proving, dot with 4 tablespoons pesto and pile the asparagus on top. Drizzle with olive oil and salt to serve.

sour cherry & almond rings

Makes **10 rings**

Time **1½–2½ hours**,
depending on machine, plus
shaping, proving and baking

Dough

1 large **egg**, beaten

150 ml (¼ pint) **milk**

75 g (3 oz) **unsalted butter**,
softened

¼ teaspoon **salt**

325 g (11 oz) **strong white
bread flour**

75 g (3 oz) **ground almonds**

50 g (2 oz) **golden caster
sugar**

1¼ teaspoons **fast-action
dried yeast**

150 g (5 oz) **dried sour
cherries**

To finish

beaten **egg**, to glaze

flaked almonds, for sprinkling

icing sugar, for dusting

Lift the bread pan out of the machine and fit the blade.
Put the dough ingredients, except the cherries, in the
pan, following the order specified in the manual.

Fit the pan into the machine and close the lid. Set to
the dough programme, adding the cherries when the
machine beeps.

At the end of the programme turn the dough out on to
a floured surface and divide it into 10 equal pieces.
Shape each piece into a ball, then press a hole through
the centre with your floured finger, gradually enlarging
the hole by rotating your finger.

Space the dough rings about 4 cm (1½ inches) apart
on 2 large, greased baking sheets. Cover loosely with
oiled clingfilm and leave to rise in a warm place until
almost doubled in size.

Brush the rings lightly with beaten egg and sprinkle
with plenty of flaked almonds. Bake in a preheated oven,
220°C (425°F), Gas Mark 7, for 10–15 minutes or until
risen and pale golden. Transfer to a wire rack to cool.
Serve dusted with icing sugar.

For pecan & apple rings, make the dough as above,
adding 1 teaspoon mixed spice and replacing the
cherries with 75 g (3 oz) chopped pecan nuts and 75 g
(3 oz) chopped dessert apple. After baking mix 100 g
(3½ oz) icing sugar with 2–3 teaspoons water to make a
loose icing and drizzle over the buns.

clementine & fig savarins

Makes **8 savarins**

Time **1½–2½ hours**,
depending on machine, plus
shaping, proving and baking

Dough

2 **eggs**, beaten

75 ml (3 fl oz) **milk**

75 g (3 oz) **unsalted butter**,
softened

¼ teaspoon **salt**

250 g (8 oz) **strong white
bread flour**

40 g (1½ oz) **golden caster
sugar**

1 teaspoon **fast-action dried
yeast**

To finish

200 g (7 oz) **golden caster
sugar**

5 tablespoons **Drambuie** or
orange-flavoured liqueur

2 tablespoons **lemon juice**

6 **clementines**, peeled and
segmented

4 fresh **figs**, each cut into
6 wedges

Lift the bread pan out of the machine and fit the blade. Put the dough ingredients in the pan, following the order specified in the manual.

Fit the pan into the machine and close the lid. Set to the dough programme.

At the end of the programme turn the dough out on to a floured surface and divide it into 8 equal pieces. Grease 8 dariole moulds or similar sized individual metal moulds. Press a piece of dough into each tin. Cover loosely with oiled clingfilm and leave to rise in a warm place until the dough reaches the tops of the tins.

Bake in a preheated oven, 220°C (425°F), Gas Mark 7, for about 15 minutes until risen and golden.

Make the syrup. Put the sugar in a medium-sized saucepan with 500 ml (17 fl oz) water and heat gently until the sugar has dissolved. Bring to the boil and boil for 5 minutes, then stir in the liqueur and lemon juice. Add the clementines and cook gently for 1 minute. Add the figs and cook for a further 30 seconds. Drain the fruits.

Remove the savarins from the tins and spoon 2 tablespoons of the syrup over each. Boil the remaining syrup and reduced it by about half so that is very syrupy. Leave to cool.

Arrange the savarins and fruits on serving plates and spoon over the syrup to serve.

salt & pepper crusted rolls

Makes **12 rolls**

Time **1½–2½ hours**,
   depending on machine, plus
   shaping, proving and baking

275 ml (9 fl oz) **water**

25 g (1 oz) **unsalted butter**,
   softened

475 g (15 oz) **strong white
   bread flour**

1 teaspoon **caster sugar**

1¼ teaspoons **fast-action
   dried yeast**

2 teaspoons **sea salt**

2 teaspoons **multi-coloured
   peppercorns**, crushed

1 tablespoon **semolina flour**

milk, to brush

Lift the bread pan out of the machine and fit the blade. Add the water, butter, flour, sugar, yeast and ½ teaspoon of the salt to the pan, following the order specified in the manual.

Fit the pan into the machine and close the lid. Set to the dough programme.

Mix the remaining salt with the pepper and semolina and sprinkle on a plate.

At the end of the programme turn the dough out on to a floured surface and cut it into 12 equal pieces. Shape each into a ball and brush the tops lightly with milk. Dip in the salt and pepper mixture and then space them about 4 cm (1½ inches) apart on a large, greased baking sheet. Cover loosely with a clean, dry tea towel and leave to rise in a warm place for 30 minutes.

Bake in a preheated oven, 220°C (425°F), Gas Mark 7, for about 10 minutes until risen and golden. Transfer to a wire rack to cool.

For floury baps, make the dough as above, increasing the salt in the dough to 1 teaspoon and using milk instead of water. At the end of the programme divide the dough into 8 equal pieces and shape each into a flat oval, about 1 cm (½ inch) thick. Place on a floured baking sheet. Brush lightly with milk and dust with plenty of flour. Leave to prove, uncovered, for 30 minutes. Make a deep impression in the centre of each bap and bake as above until golden around the edges.

devonshire splits

Makes **12 splits**

Time **1½–2½ hours**, depending on machine, plus shaping, proving and baking

Dough

300 ml (½ pint) **cold water**

2 tablespoons **butter**, at room temperature

½ teaspoon **salt**

2 tablespoons **milk powder**

500 g (1 lb) **strong white bread flour**

2 teaspoons **caster sugar**

1¼ teaspoons **fast-action dried yeast**

To finish

beaten **egg**, to glaze

250 g (8 oz) **strawberry jam**

250 g (8 oz) **clotted cream**

icing sugar, for dusting

Lift the bread pan out of the machine and fit the blade. Put the dough ingredients in the pan, following the order specified in the manual.

Fit the pan into the machine and close the lid. Set to the dough programme.

At the end of the programme turn the dough out on to a floured surface and cut it into 12 pieces. Shape each piece into a ball. Put them on large, greased baking sheets, leaving a little space around each one. Cover loosely with oiled clingfilm and leave to rise in a warm place for 20–30 minutes.

Brush the rolls with beaten egg. Bake in a preheated oven, 200°C (400°F), Gas Mark 6, for 10 minutes until golden and the bases sound hollow when tapped with the fingertips. Transfer to a wire rack to cool.

When ready to serve, cut a diagonal slice down through the rolls almost but not quite through to the base. Spoon the jam into the slit, then add spoonfuls of clotted cream. Transfer to serving plates and dust with icing sugar.

For lemon splits, make and bake the dough as above, adding the finely grated rind of 2 lemons to the dough. To finish, slice the rolls as above and fill with lightly whipped cream and lemon curd.

apple & ginger coils

Makes **12 coils**

Time **1½–2½ hours**,
depending on machine, plus
shaping, proving and baking

Dough

2 **eggs**, beaten

175 ml (6 fl oz) **milk**

2 tablespoons **butter**, at room
temperature

½ teaspoon **salt**

500 g (1 lb) **strong white
bread flour**

50 g (2 oz) **caster sugar**

1¼ teaspoons **fast-action
dried yeast**

Filling

400 g (13 oz) **cooking
apples**, peeled and cored

1 tablespoon **lemon juice**

2 tablespoons **water**

50 g (2 oz) **caster sugar**

125 g (4 oz) **luxury mixed
dried fruit**

2 tablespoons ready-chopped
glacé ginger

To finish

2 tablespoons **caster sugar**

4 tablespoons **milk**

icing sugar, for dusting

Lift the bread pan out of the machine and fit the blade.
Put the dough ingredients in the pan, following the
order specified in the manual. Fit the pan into the
machine and close the lid. Set to the dough programme.

Meanwhile, make the filling. Dice the apples and place
in a small saucepan with the lemon juice, water, sugar
and dried fruit. Cover and simmer for 5 minutes until
they are just beginning to soften. Remove the lid and
cook for 3–5 minutes more until the liquid has
evaporated and the apples are tender and the dried
fruits are plumped up. Stir in the ginger; leave to cool.

At the end of the programme turn the dough out on to
a floured surface. Roll it out to a rectangle, 38 x 30 cm
(15 x 12 inches).

Spread the apple mixture over the dough to within
about 2 cm (¾ inch) of the edges. Roll it up, starting
from one of the longer edges.

Cut the dough into 12 thick slices and arrange the
pieces, cut sides up, in 3 rows of 4 coils in a buttered
roasting tin, with a base measurement of 30 x 20 cm
(12 x 8 inches). Cover loosely with oiled clingfilm and
leave to rise in a warm place for 30 minutes.

Bake in a preheated oven, 200°C (400°F), Gas Mark 6,
for 20–25 minutes until golden and the central coils
sound hollow when tapped. When they are almost
ready, make the glaze by heating together the sugar
and milk until the sugar has dissolved. Boil for 1
minute, then brush over the hot bread. Dust with the
icing sugar.

party
breads

ciambella mandorlata

Makes **1 large loaf**
  (about 15 thick slices)
Time **1½–2½ hours**,
  depending on machine, plus
  shaping, proving and baking

Dough
2 **eggs**, beaten
100 ml (3½ fl oz) **milk**
finely grated rind of 2 **lemons**,
  plus 3 tablespoons juice
75 g (3 oz) **unsalted butter**,
  softened
1 teaspoon **salt**
½ teaspoon **ground cinnamon**
450 g (14½ oz) **strong white**
  bread flour
75 g (3 oz) **caster sugar**
1½ teaspoons **fast-action**
  dried yeast

To finish
15 g (½ oz) **unsalted butter**,
  melted and cooled
1 teaspoon **ground cinnamon**
3 tablespoons **caster sugar**
100 g (3½ oz) **blanched**
  almonds, finely chopped
1 **egg yolk**, to glaze

Lift the bread pan out of the machine and fit the blade. Put the dough ingredients in the pan, following the order specified in the manual. Add the lemon rind and juice with the milk.

Fit the pan into the machine and close the lid. Set to the dough programme.

Put the melted butter in a bowl and stir in the cinnamon, sugar and almonds until evenly mixed.

At the end of the programme turn the dough out on to a floured surface and cut it in half. Roll each half into a thick rope about 45 cm (18 inches) long. Twist the ropes together and transfer to a large, greased and lined baking sheet, curving the ends round into a crescent shape. Cover loosely with oiled clingfilm and leave to rise in a warm place for 50–60 minutes or until risen by at least half again.

Mix the egg yolk with 1 teaspoon water and brush over the dough. Scatter with the almond mixture, pressing it gently into the dough. Bake in a preheated oven, 200°C (400°F), Gas Mark 6, for about 35 minutes until deep golden, covering with foil if the bread starts to over-brown. Transfer to a wire rack to cool.

For walnut & orange praline plait, make the dough as above, using orange rind and juice instead of the lemon. For the topping, use chopped walnuts instead of the almonds and light muscovado sugar instead of the caster sugar. Finish as above.

greek easter wreath

Makes **1 large loaf** (about
   15 chunky slices)
Time **1½–2½ hours**,
   depending on machine, plus
   shaping, proving and baking

Dough
2 **eggs**, beaten
200 ml (7 fl oz) **milk**
3 tablespoons **brandy**
50 g (2 oz) **unsalted butter**,
   melted
½ teaspoon **salt**
2 teaspoons **caraway seeds**
625 g (1¼ lb) **strong white
   bread flour**
25 g (1 oz) **caster sugar**
2 teaspoons **fast-action dried
   yeast**

To finish
beaten **egg**, to glaze
1 **egg white**
2 teaspoons **caster sugar**
5 **hard-boiled eggs**, painted
   red with food colouring
50 g (2 oz) whole **blanched
   almonds**

Lift the bread pan out of the machine and fit the blade.
Put the dough ingredients in the pan, following the order
specified in the manual. Add the brandy with the milk.

Fit the pan into the machine and close the lid. Set to
the dough programme.

At the end of the programme turn the dough out on
to a floured surface. Cut it into 3 equal pieces and roll
each piece to a rope, about 50 cm (20 inches) long.
Plait the 3 ropes together and carefully transfer to a
large, greased baking sheet, bending the ends round
to form a circular, plaited ball of dough. Brush the top
lightly with beaten egg. Cover loosely with oiled
clingfilm and leave to rise in a warm place for about
45 minutes or until almost doubled in size.

Mix the egg white with the sugar and brush all over
the dough. Press the hard-boiled eggs gently into the
top of the dough and decorate with the almonds. Bake
in a preheated oven, 200°C (400°F), Gas Mark 6, for
about 50 minutes until the dough sounds hollow when
tapped with the fingertips. Cover with foil during
baking if the surface starts to over-brown. Transfer to
a wire rack to cool.

For honey butter, to accompany the toasted bread
for breakfast, put 100 g (3½ oz) softened unsalted
butter in a bowl and beat until smooth. Add 150 g
(5 oz) set honey and beat well until evenly mixed.
Turn into a small dish and chill until ready to serve.

148

stollen

Makes **1 small loaf** (about 10 thick slices)

Time **1½–2½ hours**, depending on machine, plus shaping, proving and baking

Dough

200 ml (7 fl oz) **milk**

finely grated rind of 1 **lemon**

50 g (2 oz) **unsalted butter**, softened

½ teaspoon **salt**

½ teaspoon **ground mixed spice**

350 g (11½ oz) **strong white bread flour**

50 g (2 oz) **golden caster sugar**

1¼ teaspoons **fast-action dried yeast**

75 g (3 oz) **sultanas**

50 g (2 oz) **blanched hazelnuts**, chopped

50 g (2 oz) **candied peel**, chopped

To finish

250 g (8 oz) **hazelnut marzipan** (see below) or **almond marzipan** (see pages 184–5)

icing sugar, for dusting

Lift the bread pan out of the machine and fit the blade. Put the dough ingredients, except the sultanas, nuts and peel, in the pan, following the order specified in the manual.

Fit the pan into the machine and close the lid. Set to the dough programme, adding the sultanas, hazelnuts and peel when the machine beeps.

Roll the marzipan into a thick log about 25 cm (10 inches) long.

At the end of the programme turn the dough out on to a floured surface and roll it out to an oval, about 30 x 18 cm (12 x 7 inches). Lay the log of marzipan over the dough slightly to one side of the centre. Brush a long edge with a little water and fold the wider piece of dough over the filling, pressing it down gently.

Transfer the stollen to a large, greased baking sheet and cover loosely with oiled clingfilm. Leave to rise in a warm place until almost doubled in size. Bake in a preheated oven, 200°C (400°F), Gas Mark 6, for about 25 minutes until risen and golden. Transfer to a wire rack to cool. Dust generously with icing sugar before serving.

For homemade hazelnut marzipan, grind 150 g (5 oz) whole blanched hazelnuts in a food processor. Add 50 g (2 oz) caster sugar and 50 g (2 oz) icing sugar to the processor and blend briefly to mix. Add 1 small egg white and blend until the mixture comes together to make a paste. Gather into a ball, wrap in clingfilm and keep in a cool place until ready to use.

challah

Makes **1 large loaf**

Time **1½–2½ hours**,
    depending on machine, plus
    shaping, proving and baking

Dough

175 ml (6 fl oz) **water**

2 **eggs**, beaten

50 g (2 oz) **unsalted butter**,
    melted

3 tablespoons **clear honey**

1 teaspoon **salt**

500 g (1 lb) **strong white
    bread flour**

1¼ teaspoons **fast-action
    dried yeast**

To finish

1 **egg yolk**, to glaze

2 teaspoons **poppy seeds**,
    for sprinkling

Lift the bread pan out of the machine and fit the blade. Put the dough ingredients in the pan, following the order specified in the manual.

Fit the pan into the machine and close the lid. Set to the dough programme.

At the end of the programme turn the dough out on to a floured surface. Shape it into a thick rope about 73 cm (29 inches) long. Coil up loosely and put it into a 20 cm (8 inch) greased springform tin. Cover loosely with oiled clingfilm and leave in a warm place for 45 minutes or until the dough reaches the top of the tin.

Mix the egg yolk with 1 tablespoon of water and brush the surface of the dough. Sprinkle with the poppy seeds and bake in a preheated oven, 200°C (400°F), Gas Mark 6, for 30 minutes until the bread is deep brown and sounds hollow when tapped with the fingertips. Check after 10 minutes and cover with foil if over-browning. Transfer to a wire rack to cool.

For enriched poppy seed & lemon loaf, toast 50 g (2 oz) poppy seeds in a small, dry frying pan until they start to pop. Put in the bread pan with 100 ml (3½ fl oz) water, 75 ml (3 fl oz) lemon juice, the grated rind of 1 lemon, 2 large eggs, 50 g (2 oz) very soft unsalted butter, ½ teaspoon salt, 450 g (14½ oz) strong white bread flour, 50 g (2 oz) caster sugar and 1¼ teaspoons fast-action dried yeast, following the order specified in the manual. Set to a 750 g (1½ lb) loaf size on a basic white programme. Just before baking brush the dough lightly with milk and scatter with extra poppy seeds.

panettone

Makes **1 large loaf**
Time **1½–2½ hours**,
   depending on machine, plus
   shaping, proving and baking

1 large **egg**, beaten
200 ml (7 fl oz) **milk**
finely grated rind of 1 **lemon**
finely grated rind of 1 **orange**
2 teaspoons **vanilla bean
   paste** or **vanilla extract**
50 g (2 oz) **unsalted butter**,
   softened
½ teaspoon **salt**
½ teaspoon **ground nutmeg**
500 g (1 lb) **strong white
   bread flour**
100 g (3½ oz) **caster sugar**
1½ teaspoons **fast-action
   dried yeast**
200 g (7 oz) luxury **mixed
   dried fruit**
icing sugar, for dusting
   (optional)

Lift the bread pan out of the machine and fit the blade. Put the ingredients, except the dried fruit, in the pan, following the order specified in the manual.

Fit the pan into the machine and close the lid. Set to the dough programme, checking the consistency of the dough after about 5 minutes kneading. If the dough is soft and sticky add a little more flour. Add the dried fruit when the machine beeps.

Grease a 15 cm (6 inch) round cake tin, at least 9 cm (3½ inches) deep. Line the sides with a triple thickness of baking parchment so that it extends 5 cm (2 inches) above the rim. Grease the paper.

At the end of the programme turn the dough out on to a floured surface and shape it into a ball. Drop the ball into the tin. Cover loosely with oiled clingfilm and leave to rise in a warm place until the dough reaches the top of the paper.

Bake in a preheated oven, 200°C (400°F), Gas Mark 6, for about 30 minutes or until risen and golden, covering with foil if the surface starts to over-brown. Shake the bread out of the tin and tap the base; it should sound hollow. If necessary, cook a little longer.

Transfer to a wire rack to cool. Serve dusted with icing sugar (if liked).

For pandolce, chop 150 g (5 oz) candied citrus peel into small pieces. Roughly chop 50 g (2 oz) blanched almonds. Make the dough as above, using candied peel and nuts instead of the mixed dried fruit. Shape the dough and finish as above.

hot cross buns

Makes **12 buns**

Time 1½–2½ **hours**,
depending on machine, plus
shaping, proving and baking

Dough

1 **egg**, beaten

275 ml (9 fl oz) **milk**

40 g (1½ oz) **unsalted butter**,
softened

½ teaspoon **salt**

2 teaspoons **ground mixed
spice**

500 g (1 lb) **strong white
bread flour**

3 tablespoons **light
muscovado sugar**

1½ teaspoons **fast-action
dried yeast**

100g (3½ oz) **raisins**

To finish

50 g (2 oz) **plain flour**

4 tablespoons **milk**

2 tablespoons **caster sugar**

Lift the bread pan out of the machine and fit the blade.
Add the dough ingredients, except the raisins, to the
pan, following the order specified in the manual.

Fit the pan into the machine and close the lid. Set to
the dough programme, adding the raisins when the
machine beeps.

At the end of the programme turn the dough out on
to a floured surface and divide it into 12 pieces. Shape
each into a ball and space 5 cm (2 inches) apart on a
greased baking sheet. Cover loosely with oiled clingfilm
and leave to rise in a warm place for 30 minutes.

Make the crosses. Beat 4–5 tablespoons water into
the flour to make a paste. Put it in a greaseproof piping
bag (or spoon it into the corner of a small polythene
bag) and snip off the tip. Pipe crosses over the buns.

Bake in a preheated oven, 220°C (425°F), Gas Mark 7,
for 15 minutes until risen and golden. Heat the milk and
sugar in a pan until the sugar dissolves. Bring to the
boil and brush over the buns. Cool on a wire rack.

For hot cross bun loaf, put 275 ml (9 fl oz) milk,
25 g (1 oz) very soft butter, ½ teaspoon salt, finely
grated rind of 1 lemon, 2 teaspoons ground mixed
spice, 450 g (14½ oz) strong white bread flour, 50 g
(2 oz) light muscovado sugar and 1½ teaspoons fast-
action dried yeast in the bread pan, following the order
specified in the manual. Set to a 750g (1½ lb) loaf size
on the sweet programme, adding 225 g (7½ oz) luxury
mixed dried fruit when the machine beeps. Halfway
through baking, pipe a cross on the surface using the
mixture above. After baking brush with the glaze.

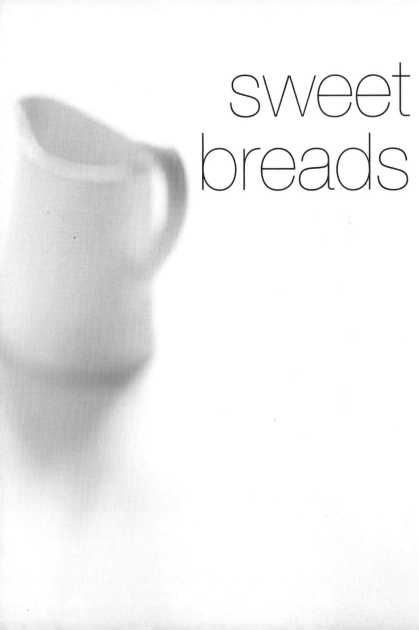

sweet breads

sweet pineapple & lime loaf

Makes **1 medium loaf**
  (about 8 thick slices)
Time **1½–2½ hours**,
  depending on machine, plus
  shaping, proving and baking

Dough
200 ml (7 fl oz) **water**
25 g (1 oz) **unsalted butter**,
  softened
½ teaspoon **five spice powder**
finely grated rind of 2 **limes**,
  plus 4 tablespoons juice
½ teaspoon **salt**
400 g (13 oz) **strong white
  bread flour**
65 g (2½ oz) **caster sugar**
¾ teaspoon **fast-action dried
  yeast**

To finish
300 g (10 oz) sweetened
  semi-dried pineapple,
  chopped into small pieces
75 g (3 oz) **icing sugar**
pared **lime rind**, for sprinkling

Lift the bread pan out of the machine and fit the blade. Put the water, butter, five spice powder, lime rind, 3 tablespoons lime juice, salt, flour, sugar and yeast in the pan, following the order specified in the manual. Fit the pan into the machine and close the lid. Set to the dough programme.

At the end of the programme turn the dough out on to a floured surface and divide it into 4 pieces. Grease a 1 kg (2 lb) loaf tin and line the base and long sides with a strip of greaseproof paper. Flatten each piece of dough to a rectangle that is roughly the size of the tin and place a piece in the base. Scatter with one quarter of the chopped pineapple. Cover with a second layer of dough. Repeat the layering, finishing with a layer of fruit. Cover loosely with oiled clingfilm and leave to rise in a warm place until almost doubled in size.

Bake in a preheated oven, 200°C (400°F), Gas Mark 6, for 30 minutes or until risen and golden. Turn out of the tin and return to the oven for a further 5–10 minutes or until the loaf sounds hollow when tapped with the fingertips. Cover with foil if the loaf starts to over-brown.

Mix the icing sugar with the remaining lime juice and drizzle over the bread. Sprinkle with lime rind; let cool.

For pear & ginger loaf with lemon glaze, make the dough as above, using ground ginger instead of the five spice powder and lemon rind and juice instead of lime. Chop 300 g (10 oz) dried pears. Layer the dough and pears in the tin. Bake as above. Mix the icing sugar with 1 tablespoon lemon juice and drizzle over the bread.

sticky toffee & date loaf

Makes **1 large loaf**
Time **2¾–3½ hours**,
  depending on machine, plus
  cooking

250 g (8 oz) pitted **dates**,
  roughly chopped
300 g (10 oz) **toffee sauce**
  (see below)
1 large **egg**, beaten
175 ml (6 fl oz) **milk**
50 g (2 oz) **unsalted butter**,
  softened
¼ teaspoon **salt**
1½ teaspoons **ground mixed
  spice**
400 g (13 oz) **strong white
  bread flour**
1¼ teaspoons **fast-action
  dried yeast**
icing sugar, for dusting

Put the dates in a small saucepan with 5 tablespoons water. Cover and cook gently for about 5 minutes until the dates have softened and the water has been absorbed. Leave to cool.

Lift the bread pan out of the machine and fit the blade. Put 150 g (5 oz) of the toffee sauce in the pan with the remaining ingredients, except the dates, following the order specified in the manual.

Fit the pan into the machine and close the lid. Set to a 750 g (1½ lb) loaf size on the sweet programme (or basic if the machine doesn't have a sweet setting). Add the dates to the pan when the machine beeps.

At the end of the programme lift the pan out of the machine and shake the bread out on to a wire rack to cool. Dust with icing sugar. Serve freshly baked or lightly toasted with the remaining sauce spooned over. If the sauce has become very thick on cooling, it can be heated gently to soften.

For homemade toffee sauce, put 150 ml (¼ pint) double cream in a saucepan with 175 g (6 oz) light muscovado sugar and 75 g (3 oz) unsalted butter. Heat gently, stirring, until the sugar has dissolved and the butter melted. Bring to the boil and let the sauce bubble for 5–8 minutes until the mixture thickens and darkens. Turn into a bowl and leave to cool before using.

blueberry & vanilla plait

Makes **1 large plait** (about
  10 thick slices)
Time **1½–2½ hours**, depending
  on machine, plus shaping,
  proving and baking

Dough
150 ml (¼ pint) **water**
2 teaspoons **vanilla bean
  paste**
1 large **egg**, beaten
75 g (3 oz) **unsalted butter**,
  softened
¼ teaspoon **salt**
350 g (11½ oz) **strong white
  bread flour**
50 g (2 oz) **ground almonds**
50 g (2 oz) **caster sugar**
1¼ teaspoons **fast-action
  dried yeast**

To finish
125 g (4 oz) **ricotta cheese**
250 g (8 oz) **blueberries**
3 tablespoons **caster sugar**
beaten **egg**, to glaze
vanilla sugar, for sprinkling

Lift the bread pan out of the machine and fit the blade.
Put the dough ingredients in the pan, following the
order specified in the manual. The vanilla bean paste
should be added with the liquids and the almonds with
the flour. Fit the pan into the machine and close the lid.
Set to the dough programme.

At the end of the programme turn the dough out on to
a floured surface and divide it into 3 equal pieces. Roll
each piece to a strip about 35 x 12 cm (14 x 5 inches).
Spread ricotta over each strip to about 2 cm (¾ inch) of
the edges. Scatter with 200 g (7 oz) of the blueberries
and sprinkle 1 tablespoon sugar over each strip. Bring
up the edges over the filling, pinching them together
firmly to make 3 thick ropes. Roll them over so the
joins are underneath. Plait the strips together, tucking
the ends underneath, and carefully lift on to a large,
greased baking sheet. Cover loosely with oiled clingfilm
and leave to rise in a warm place for 40 minutes or
until nearly doubled in size.

Brush with beaten egg. Scatter with the remaining
blueberries and sprinkle with vanilla sugar. Bake in a
preheated oven, 200°C (400°F), Gas Mark 6, for 30
minutes or until risen and golden. Cool on a wire rack.

For red fruit & vanilla loaf, make and shape the
dough as above. Use cream cheese instead of the
ricotta and 200 g (7 oz) mixed dried red fruit (such as
cranberries, sour cherries and strawberries) instead of
the blueberries. Before cooking scatter with an extra
50 g (2 oz) chopped red fruits and sprinkle with
vanilla sugar.

coffee & walnut bread

Makes **1 large loaf**

Time **2¾–3½ hours**,
  depending on machine

2 tablespoons **espresso
  coffee powder**
1 large **egg**, beaten
50 g (2 oz) **unsalted butter**,
  melted
¼ teaspoon **salt**
350 g (11½ oz) **strong white
  bread flour**
50 g (2 oz) **light muscovado
  sugar**
1¼ teaspoons **fast-action
  dried yeast**
75 g (3 oz) **walnut pieces**,
  lightly toasted

Blend the coffee with 150 ml (¼ pint) boiling water and leave to cool. Lift the bread pan out of the machine and fit the blade. Put the ingredients, except the walnuts, in the pan, following the order specified in the manual.

Fit the pan into the machine and close the lid. Set to a 750 g (1½ lb) loaf size on the sweet programme (or basic if the machine doesn't have a sweet setting). Add the walnuts to the pan when the machine beeps.

At the end of the programme lift the pan out of the machine and shake the bread out on to a wire rack to cool.

For maple butter, to spread over the freshly baked bread, whisk together 100 g (3½ oz) soft unsalted butter, 4 tablespoons icing sugar and 1 teaspoon vanilla bean paste or vanilla extract until completely smooth. Beat in 5 tablespoons maple syrup until combined. Turn into a small serving dish and chill until ready to serve.

rich fruit teabread

Makes **1 extra-large loaf**

Time **1½–2½ hours**,
    depending on machine, plus
    shaping, proving and baking

175 ml (6 fl oz) strong **black
    tea**, cooled
1 **egg**, beaten
50 g (2 oz) **unsalted butter**,
    softened
½ teaspoon **salt**
finely grated rind of **1 orange**
1 tablespoon **ground mixed
    spice**
375 g (12 oz) **strong white
    bread flour**
75 g (3 oz) **dark muscovado
    sugar**
1½ teaspoons **fast-action
    dried yeast**
200 g (7 oz) luxury **mixed
    dried fruit**
100 g (3½ oz) ready-to-eat
    dried apricots, roughly
    chopped
100 g (3½ oz) **Brazil nuts**,
    chopped
demerara sugar, for sprinkling

Lift the bread pan out of the machine and fit the blade. Put the ingredients, except the dried fruit and nuts, in the pan, following the order specified in the manual. Add the spice with the flour.

Fit the pan in the machine and close the lid. Set to the dough programme, adding the dried fruits and nuts when the machine beeps.

At the end of the programme turn the dough out on to a floured surface and shape it into an oval. Grease a 1 kg (2 lb) loaf tin and drop the dough into the tin. Cover loosely with oiled clingfilm and leave to rise in a warm place for 50–60 minutes or until almost doubled in size.

Sprinkle generously with demerara sugar and bake in a preheated oven, 220°C (425°F), Gas Mark 7, for 35–40 minutes until risen and golden. Cover the top with foil if the surface starts to over-brown. Turn out of the tin and tap the base: it should sound hollow. If necessary, return to the oven (out of the tin) for a little longer.

For chunky fruit & nut loaf, put 1 egg, 175 ml (6 fl oz) milk, 50 g (2 oz) very soft butter, 1 tablespoon black treacle, ½ teaspoon salt, 375 g (12 oz) strong white bread flour, 1 tablespoon ground mixed spice, 50 g (2 oz) dark muscovado sugar and 1¼ teaspoons fast-action dried yeast in the bread pan, following the order specified in the manual. Set to the sweet programme. Add 150 g (5 oz) luxury mixed dried fruit and 75 g (3 oz) roughly chopped almonds when the machine beeps. At the end of the programme shake the bread out on to a wire rack to cool.

white chocolate & banana loaf

Makes **1 large loaf**
Time **1–2 hours**, depending
  on machine

225 g (7½ oz) mashed
  banana (about 2 large
  bananas)
150 ml (¼ pint) warm **milk**
50 g (2 oz) **unsalted butter**,
  softened
½ teaspoon **salt**
425 g (14 oz) **strong white
  bread flour**
50 g (2 oz) **caster sugar**
2½ teaspoons **fast-action
  dried yeast**
200 g (7 oz) **white chocolate**,
  chopped
100 g (3½ oz) **pecan nuts**,
  roughly chopped
icing sugar, for dusting

Lift the bread pan out of the machine and fit the blade.
Put the ingredients, except the chocolate and nuts, in
the pan, following the order specified in the manual.
Add the mashed banana with the milk.

Fit the pan into the machine and close the lid. Set to
a 750 g (1½ lb) loaf size on the fast/rapid bake
programme. Add the chocolate and pecans when the
machine beeps.

At the end of the programme lift the pan out of the
machine and shake the bread out on to a wire rack to
cool. Serve dusted with icing sugar.

For dark chocolate & ginger rolls, put the ingredients
in the bread machine as above, replacing 25 g (1 oz)
of the flour with 25 g (1 oz) cocoa powder. Reduce
the yeast to 1½ teaspoons and add 3 pieces of stem
ginger from a jar, finely chopped. Use chopped plain
dark chocolate instead of the white. Set to the dough
programme, adding the chocolate and nuts when the
machine beeps. At the end of the programme turn out
the dough and shape into 8 small balls. Space well
apart on a greased baking sheet and cover loosely
with oiled clingfilm. Leave in a warm place to rise until
almost doubled in size. Bake in a preheated oven,
220°C (425°F), Gas Mark 7, for about 15 minutes
until risen and lightly browned. Transfer to a wire rack
to cool and serve dusted with icing sugar.

sticky chelsea buns

Makes **12 buns**
Time **1½–2½ hours**,
   depending on machine, plus
   shaping, proving and baking

Dough
1 egg, beaten
225 ml (7½ fl oz) **milk**
50 g (2 oz) **unsalted butter**,
   softened
½ teaspoon **salt**
finely grated rind of **1 lemon**
500 g (1 lb) **strong white**
   bread flour
75 g (3 oz) **caster sugar**
1½ teaspoon **fast-action dried**
   yeast

To finish
50 g (2 oz) **unsalted butter**,
   softened
50 g (2 oz) **light muscovado**
   sugar
1 teaspoon **ground mixed**
   spice
200 g (7 oz) luxury **mixed**
   dried fruit
25 g (1 oz) **fresh root ginger**,
   grated
50 g (2 oz) **caster sugar**

Lift the bread pan out of the machine and fit the blade. Put the dough ingredients in the pan, following the order specified in the manual. Fit the pan into the machine and close the lid. Set to the dough programme.

Mix together the butter and muscovado sugar to make a paste. Toss the spice with the fruit and ginger in a bowl.

At the end of the programme turn the dough out on to a floured surface and roll it out to a rectangle, about 45 x 25 cm (18 x 10 inches). Spread to the edges with the butter and sugar paste and scatter over the fruit mixture. Roll up the dough starting from a long side. Use a sharp knife to cut the log into 12 equal slices.

Grease a shallow 28 x 18 cm (11 x 7 inch) baking tin. Arrange the slices in the tin, spacing them evenly and with the cut sides up. Cover loosely with oiled clingfilm and leave to rise in a warm place for about 45 minutes or until doubled in size.

Bake in a preheated oven, 200°C (400°F), Gas Mark 6, for 25–35 minutes until risen and golden. Cover the buns with foil if they start to over-brown.

Meanwhile, put the caster sugar in a pan with 100 ml (3½ fl oz) water and heat gently until the sugar dissolves. Bring to the boil and boil for 1 minute. Transfer the buns to a wire rack and brush them with syrup. Leave to cool.

For chocolate, fruit & nut buns, substitute lemon rind for orange. Replace the butter paste and fruit mixture with 200 g (7 oz) chopped chocolate, 1 teaspoon ground ginger, 125 g (4 oz) raisins and 75 g (3 oz) chopped hazelnuts. Drizzle with melted chocolate.

soured cream & berry bread

Makes **1 large loaf**
Time **2¾–3½ hours**,
  depending on machine

150 ml (¼ pint) **water**
150 g (5 oz) full-fat **crème
  fraîche**
½ teaspoon **salt**
grated rind of **1 lemon**
425 g (14 oz) **strong white
  bread flour**
3 tablespoons **caster sugar**
1 teaspoon **fast-action dried
  yeast**
100 g (3½ oz) mixed **dried
  cherries, blueberries** and
  cranberries

Lift the bread pan out of the machine and fit the blade.
Put the ingredients, except the mixed fruit, in the pan,
following the order specified in the manual.

Fit the pan into the machine and close the lid. Set to a
750 g (1½ lb) loaf size on the sweet programme (or
basic if the machine does not have a sweet setting).
Add the dried fruits when the machine beeps.

At the end of the programme lift the pan from the
machine and shake the bread out on to a wire rack
to cool.

For berry bread with orange liqueur, put the mixed
dried berries in a bowl and pierce all over with a fork.
Add 3 tablespoons Cointreau or other orange-flavoured
liqueur to the bowl. Cover and leave to steep for
about 3 hours until the liqueur has been absorbed.
Continue to make the bread as above, using the
grated rind of 1 orange instead of the lemon.

chocolate & pecan spiral

Makes **1 extra-large loaf**

Time **1½–2½ hours**,
depending on machine, plus
shaping, proving and baking

Dough

2 **eggs**, beaten

175 ml (6 fl oz) **milk**

45 g (1¾ oz) **unsalted butter**,
softened

½ teaspoon **salt**

500 g (1 lb) **strong white
bread flour**

50 g (2 oz) **caster sugar**

1½ teaspoons **fast-action
dried yeast**

To finish

125 g (4 oz) **plain dark
chocolate**, finely chopped

125 g (4 oz) **pecan nuts**,
roughly chopped

2 tablespoons **caster sugar**

1 **egg yolk**, to glaze

Lift the bread pan out of the machine and fit the blade. Put the dough ingredients in the pan, following the order specified in the manual.

Fit the pan into the machine and close the lid. Set to the dough programme.

At the end of the programme turn the dough out on to a floured surface and roll it to a 28 cm (11 inch) square. Sprinkle over three-quarters of the chocolate and the nuts and all of the sugar. Roll up the dough, then put it into a greased 1.8 litre (3 pint) loaf tin. Cover loosely with oiled clingfilm and leave in a warm place for 30 minutes or until the dough reaches just above the top of the tin.

Mix the egg yolk with 1 tablespoon of water and brush it over the dough. Sprinkle over the remaining chocolate and pecan nuts and bake in a preheated oven, 200°C (400°F), Gas Mark 6, for 35–40 minutes until the bread is well risen and deep brown and sounds hollow when tapped with the fingertips. Cover with foil after 10 minutes to prevent the nuts from over-browning.

For brandied prune & chocolate slice, roughly chop 200 g (7 oz) soft pitted prunes and put them in a bowl with 2 tablespoons brandy and steep for 2 hours. Make the dough as above. Turn the dough out on to a floured surface and work in the prunes and 100 g (3½ oz) each of plain and white chocolate. Shape into a log and drop into a greased 1.8 litre (3 pint) loaf tin. Cover loosely with oiled clingfilm and leave in a warm place until almost doubled in size. Bake as above. After baking, dust with a mixture of cocoa powder and icing sugar.

poppy seed, orange & fig loaf

Makes **1 large loaf**

Time **3–4 hours**, depending on machine

4 tablespoons **poppy seeds**, plus extra for sprinkling

2 **oranges**

1 large **egg**, beaten

50 g (2 oz) **unsalted butter**, softened

425 g (14 oz) **strong white bread flour**

4 tablespoons **light muscovado sugar**

1¼ teaspoons **fast-action dried yeast**

200 g (7 oz) **dried figs** (stalks removed), halved

50 g (2 oz) **candied orange**, chopped

milk, to brush

Lightly toast the poppy seeds in a dry frying pan. Grate the rind from the oranges and squeeze the juice. Make the juice up to 225 ml (7½ fl oz) with water.

Lift the bread pan out of the machine and fit the blade. Put the ingredients, except the figs and candied orange, in the pan, following the order specified in the manual.

Fit the pan into the machine and close the lid. Set to a 750 g (1½ lb) loaf size on the basic white programme. Select your preferred crust setting. Add the figs and candied orange when the machine beeps.

Just before baking begins brush the top of the dough lightly with milk and sprinkle with extra poppy seeds. Close the lid gently.

At the end of the programme lift the pan out of the machine and shake the bread out on to a wire rack to cool. Serve freshly baked and buttered.

For seeded banana loaf, cut 200 g (7 oz) chewy dried banana slices in half. Lightly toast 4 tablespoons sunflower seeds. Make the loaf as above, substituting the sunflower seeds for poppy seeds and the bananas for the figs. Add 2 teaspoons ground mixed spice with the flour.

178

pine nut, lemon & cardamom loaf

Makes **1 medium loaf**
Time **1½–2½ hours**,
    depending on machine, plus
    shaping, proving and baking

Dough
20 **cardamom pods**
finely grated rind and juice
    of 2 **lemons**
1 large **egg**, beaten
50 g (2 oz) **unsalted butter**,
    softened
½ teaspoon **salt**
3 tablespoons **milk powder**
425 g (14 oz) **strong white**
    bread flour
50 g (2 oz) **caster sugar**
1¼ teaspoons **fast-action**
    dried yeast

To finish
150 g (5 oz) **pine nuts**,
    toasted
50 g (2 oz) **flaked almonds**
150 g (5 oz) **sultanas**
1 tablespoon **lemon juice**
65 g (2½ oz) **icing sugar**

Grind the cardamom pods using a pestle and mortar to extract the seeds. Discard the shells and grind the seeds to break them up. Put the lemon rind and juice in a measuring jug and make it up to 225 ml (7½ fl oz) with water.

Lift the bread pan out of the machine and fit the blade. Put the dough ingredients in the pan, following the order specified in the manual.

Fit the pan into the machine and close the lid. Set to the dough programme.

At the end of the programme turn the dough out on to a floured surface and knead in the pine nuts, almonds and sultanas until evenly distributed. Shape the dough into a log shape, about 25 cm (10 inches) long, and place it on a large, greased baking sheet. Cover loosely with oiled clingfilm and leave to rise in a warm place for about 45 minutes or until almost doubled in size.

Bake in a preheated oven, 220°C (425°F), Gas Mark 7, for about 25 minutes until risen and golden and the base sounds hollow when tapped. Cool on a wire rack.

Beat together the lemon juice and icing sugar to make a thin icing. Drizzle over the bread to decorate.

For orange florentine loaf, make the dough as above, using orange rind and juice instead of the lemon. Mix together 150 g (5 oz) flaked almonds, 100 g (3½ oz) natural glacé cherries, halved, 100 g (3½ oz) raisins and 1 tablespoon ground ginger. Knead into the dough instead of the pine nuts, almonds and sultanas. Once baked, drizzle with melted white chocolate.

pistachio loaf with tropical fruits

Makes **1 large loaf**

Time **2¾–3½ hours**,
  depending on machine

Dough

75 g (3 oz) shelled **pistachio
  nuts**

175 ml (6 fl oz) **mango juice**
  or **pineapple juice**

1 large **egg**

25 g (1 oz) **unsalted butter**,
  softened

½ teaspoon **salt**

425 g (14 oz) **strong white
  bread flour**

50 g (2 oz) **light muscovado
  sugar**

1¼ teaspoons **fast-action
  dried yeast**

150 g (5 oz) **semi-dried
  tropical fruits**, such as
  papaya, mango and
  pineapple, chopped

50 g (2 oz) **glacé cherries**

To finish

milk, to brush

icing sugar, for dusting

Put the pistachio nuts in a bowl and cover them with boiling water. Leave for 1 minute, then drain and rub between several layers of kitchen paper to loosen the skins. Peel away the skins and roughly chop the nuts.

Lift the bread pan out of the machine and fit the blade. Put the dough ingredients, except the nuts and fruits, in the pan, following the order specified in the manual.

Fit the pan into the machine and close the lid. Set to a 750 g (1½ lb) loaf size on the sweet programme (or basic if the machine doesn't have a sweet setting). Add the fruits and two-thirds of the pistachio nuts to the pan when the machine beeps.

Just before baking begins brush the top of the dough lightly with milk and scatter with the reserved nuts. Close the lid gently.

At the end of the programme lift the pan out of the machine and shake the bread out on to a wire rack to cool. Dust lightly with icing sugar.

For spiced rum butter, to spread over the freshly baked bread, heat 25 g (1 oz) icing sugar in a small pan with 1 teaspoon ground cinnamon and 1 tablespoon water until bubbling. Leave to cool slightly. Beat 125 g (4 oz) soft unsalted butter in a bowl. Add the cinnamon syrup, a further 50 g (2 oz) icing sugar and 2 tablespoons rum. Beat well until smooth and creamy. Turn into a small serving dish and chill until ready to serve.

nectarine & marzipan fruit kuchen

Makes **1 large loaf**
Time **1½–2½ hours**,
  depending on machine, plus
  shaping, proving and baking

Dough

150 ml (¼ pint) **water**
1 **egg**, beaten
30 g (1¼ oz) **unsalted butter**,
  softened
¼ teaspoon **salt**
1 tablespoon **milk powder**
grated rind of 1 **lemon**
300 g (10 oz) **strong white**
  bread flour
25 g (1 oz) **caster sugar**
¾ teaspoon **fast-action dried**
  yeast

To finish

125 g (4 oz) **marzipan** (see
  below), coarsely grated
500 g (1 lb) ripe **nectarines**
25 g (1 oz) **unsalted butter**,
  melted
2 tablespoons **caster sugar**
toasted **flaked almonds**, for
  sprinkling
caster sugar, for dusting

Lift the bread pan out of the machine and fit the blade. Put the dough ingredients in the pan, following the order specified in the manual.

Fit the pan into the machine and close the lid. Set to the dough programme.

At the end of the programme turn the dough out on to a floured surface. Press it into a buttered 28 cm (11 inch) fluted loose-bottomed flan tin.

Sprinkle with the grated marzipan. Halve, stone and thickly slice the nectarines and arrange them over the top. Leave to rise, uncovered, in a warm place for 40 minutes or until half as big again.

Brush the fruit with melted butter, sprinkle with sugar and bake in a preheated oven, 200°C (400°F), Gas Mark 6, for 15 minutes. Cover with foil, reduce the heat to 180°C (350°F), Gas Mark 4, and bake for a further 35–40 minutes until the base is cooked through.

Leave to stand in the tin for 10 minutes, then loosen the edges and remove the tart from the tin, keeping it on the base. Transfer to a plate, sprinkle with flaked almonds and dust with extra sugar. Serve warm.

For homemade marzipan, put 65 g (2½ oz) whole blanched almonds in a food processor and blend until finely ground. Tip into a bowl and stir in 25 g (1 oz) caster sugar, 25 g (1 oz) icing sugar, ¼ teaspoon almond or vanilla extract and 2 teaspoons egg white. Mix to a firm paste using your hands.

pear, cinnamon & raisin kugelhopf

Makes **1 ring loaf** (about 10 slices)
Time **1½–2½ hours**, depending on machine, plus shaping, proving and baking

Dough
150 ml (¼ pint) **strong cider**
1 large **egg**, beaten
75 g (3 oz) **unsalted butter**, melted
½ teaspoon **salt**
375 g (12 oz) **strong white bread flour**
50 g (2 oz) **caster sugar**
1 teaspoon **fast-action dried yeast**

To finish
50 g (2 oz) **unsalted butter**, softened
75 g (3 oz) **dark muscovado sugar**
2 teaspoons **ground cinnamon**
4 ripe **pears**
2 teaspoons **lemon juice**
100 g (3½ oz) **raisins**
icing sugar, for dusting

Lift the bread pan out of the machine and fit the blade. Put the dough ingredients in the pan, following the order specified in the manual. Fit the pan into the machine and close the lid. Set to the dough programme.

Mix the butter with the sugar and cinnamon to make a paste. Peel, core and slice the pears. Toss in the lemon juice to prevent browning.

At the end of the programme turn the dough out on to a floured surface and roll it out to a rectangle, about 35 x 25 cm (14 x 10 inches). Spread the spiced butter over the dough almost to the edges and scatter with the pears and raisins. Loosely roll up the dough. With the join facing upwards bring the ends of the dough to meet and press them together. Thoroughly grease and flour the base and sides of a 1.5 litre (2½ pint) kügelhopf tin or plain ring tin. Drop the dough into the tin.

Cover loosely with oiled clingfilm and leave to rise in a warm place for 50–60 minutes or until the dough has risen to the top of the tin.

Bake in a preheated oven, 200°C (400°F), Gas Mark 6, for about 35 minutes until risen and deep golden. Leave in the tin for 10 minutes, then loosen the edges with a knife and invert the bread on to a wire rack to cool. Serve warm or cold, dusted with icing sugar.

For spiced plum kugelhopf, halve, stone and slice 8 ripe plums. Make the kugelhopf as above, scattering the plums over the spiced butter instead of the pears. Roll up and finish as above.

summer fruit cheesecake slice

Makes **8 slices**
Time **1½–2½ hours**,
depending on machine, plus
shaping, proving and baking

Dough
1 **egg**, beaten
150 ml (¼ pint) **milk**
1 tablespoon **vanilla bean
paste** or **vanilla extract**
25 g (1 oz) **unsalted butter**,
softened
1 tablespoon **milk powder**
300 g (10 oz) **strong white
bread flour**, plus
1 tablespoon
50 g (2 oz) **caster sugar**
¾ teaspoon **fast-action dried
yeast**

To finish
200 g (7 oz) **cream cheese**
50 g (2 oz) **caster sugar**, plus
1 tablespoon for sprinkling
1 teaspoon **vanilla bean
paste** or **vanilla extract**
1 **egg**
150 g (5 oz) **raspberries**
150 g (5 oz) **strawberries**,
hulled and halved
icing sugar, for dusting

Lift the bread pan out of the machine and fit the blade.
Put the dough ingredients in the pan, following the order
specified in the manual. Fit the pan into the machine and
close the lid. Set to the dough programme.

Beat the cream cheese to soften, then beat in the
sugar, vanilla paste or extract and egg until smooth.

At the end of the programme turn the dough out on
to a floured surface and cut off one quarter. Roll out
the remainder to a round about 28 cm (11 inches) in
diameter. Grease a 23 cm (9 inch) springform cake tin.
Press the dough into the tin so that it comes about
3 cm (1¼ inches) up the sides, making a case.

Divide the remaining dough into 10 equal pieces and
scatter them into the case. Dot the cream cheese
mixture between the dough pieces, then scatter with
half the berries. Cover loosely with oiled clingfilm and
leave to rise in a warm place until slightly risen.

Bake in a preheated oven, 200°C (400°F), Gas Mark
6, for about 45 minutes until the bread is risen and
golden. Make sure the centre of the dough is cooked
by piercing it with a knife or skewer. Transfer to a wire
rack to cool. Serve scattered with the remaining fruits
and dusted with icing sugar.

For spiced peach & redcurrant slice, add

1 teaspoon ground cinnamon instead of the vanilla
paste or extract. Chop 4 ripe peaches into small
chunks and use instead of the berries. After baking,
drizzle the cake with melted redcurrant jelly and
scatter with clusters of redcurrants.

gooey chocolate nut bread

Makes **8–10 slices**

Time **1½–2½ hours,**
depending on machine, plus
shaping, proving and baking

Dough

1 large **egg**, beaten

150 ml (¼ pint) **milk**

2 teaspoons **vanilla bean paste**

75 g (3 oz) **unsalted butter,** softened

¼ teaspoon **salt**

375 g (12 oz) **strong white bread flour**

50 g (2 oz) **ground hazelnuts**

50 g (2 oz) **caster sugar**

1¼ teaspoons **fast-action dried yeast**

To finish

200 g (7 oz) **chocolate hazelnut spread**

100 g (3½ oz) **hazelnuts,** roughly chopped, plus 25 g (1 oz) to decorate

beaten **egg**, to glaze

50 g (2 oz) **plain dark chocolate,** chopped

cocoa powder and **icing sugar,** for dusting

Lift the bread pan out of the machine and fit the blade. Put the dough ingredients in the pan, following the order specified in the manual. Add the ground hazelnuts with the flour. Fit the pan into the machine and close the lid. Set to the dough programme. Grease a 20 cm (8 inch) loose-bottomed, round cake tin.

At the end of the programme turn the dough out on to a floured surface. Roll one-third of the dough to a 26 cm (10½ inch) round. Place it in the tin so it comes about 3 cm (1¼ inches) up the sides to make a case.

Dot one-third of the chocolate spread over the base and scatter with one-third of the nuts. Divide the remaining dough into 3 pieces and roll each to a 20 cm (8 inch) round. Place one layer in the tin and dot with another third of the chocolate spread and nuts. Continue layering finishing with a layer of dough.

Brush the dough with beaten egg. Press the chopped chocolate and reserved nuts into the dough. Cover loosely with oiled clingfilm and leave to rise in a warm place for 45–60 minutes or until about half the size again.

Bake in a preheated oven, 200°C (400°F), Gas Mark 6, for 50 minutes. Cover it with foil if the top starts to over-brown. Transfer to a wire rack to cool. Serve dusted with cocoa powder and icing sugar.

For white chocolate & pecan bread, instead of the chocolate spread, melt together 200 g (7 oz) white chocolate, 25 g (1 oz) unsalted butter, 1 tablespoon golden syrup and 2 tablespoons milk. Substitute pecan nuts for the hazelnuts and white chocolate for the chopped plain chocolate.

lardy cake

Makes **10 thick slices**

Time 1½–2½ hours, depending
on machine, plus shaping,
proving and baking

Dough

300 ml (½ pint) **water**

25 g (1 oz) **lard**, softened

¼ teaspoon **salt**

2 tablespoons **milk powder**

1 teaspoon **ground mixed
spice**

425 g (14 oz) **strong white
bread flour**

2 tablespoons **golden caster
sugar**

1¼ teaspoons **fast-action
dried yeast**

To finish

100 g (3½ oz) **lard**, softened

25 g (1 oz) **unsalted butter**,
softened

250 g (8 oz) **mixed dried fruit**

50 g (2 oz) chopped **candied
peel**

100 g (3½ oz) **golden caster
sugar**, plus extra for
sprinkling

milk, to brush

Lift the bread pan out of the machine and fit the blade.
Put the dough ingredients into the pan, following the
order specified in the manual.

Fit the pan into the machine and close the lid. Set to
the dough programme.

At the end of the programme turn the dough out on
to a floured surface and roll it out to a rectangle, about
40 x 23 cm (16 x 9 inches), with a short end facing
you. Using a knife, dot the lard over the dough, then
dot over smaller pieces of butter.

Mix together the dried fruit, peel and sugar and scatter
over the dough. Press down gently with your hand. Fold
the bottom third of the dough over and press down
gently, then fold the top third of the dough over to
form a rectangle of 3 layers. Turn the dough through
45 degrees and re-roll to a similar-sized rectangle. Fold
the ends in as before and re-roll to a rectangle slightly
smaller than the size of a shallow, greased 28 x 18 cm
(11 x 7 inch) baking tin. Lift the dough into the tin, cover
loosely with oiled clingfilm and leave to rise in a warm
place until risen by about half again.

Brush with a little milk and sprinkle with extra sugar.
Bake in a preheated oven, 200°C (400°F), Gas Mark 6,
for about 45 minutes until risen and golden. Leave in
the tin for 10 minutes, then transfer to a wire rack to
cool. Serve warm cut into chunky slices.

For lardy cake with ginger, grate 75 g (3 oz) fresh
root ginger and add to the pan with the water when
making the dough. Chop 50 g (2 oz) stem ginger and
mix with the dried fruit and sugar. Finish as above.

crumbly blackberry & apple torte

Makes **10 slices**

Time 1½–2½ **hours**,
depending on machine, plus
shaping, proving and baking

Dough

150 ml (¼ pint) **apple juice**

1 **egg**, beaten

25 g (1 oz) **unsalted butter**,
softened

1 tablespoon **milk powder**

½ teaspoon **ground mixed
spice**

300 g (10 oz) **strong white
bread flour**

50 g (2 oz) **caster sugar**

¾ teaspoon **fast-action dried
yeast**

To finish

50 g (2 oz) **plain flour**

40 g (1½ oz) firm **unsalted
butter**

40 g (1½ oz) **caster sugar**,
plus 2 tablespoons

600 g (1 lb 2 oz) **cooking
apples**

1 tablespoon **lemon juice**

175 g (6 oz) **blackberries**

Lift the bread pan out of the machine and fit the blade. Put the dough ingredients in the pan, following the order specified in the manual. Add the spice with the flour.

Fit the pan into the machine and close the lid. Set to the dough programme.

Blend the flour, butter and 40 g (1½ oz) sugar in a food processor until the mixture starts to bind together with a moist crumbly texture.

At the end of the programme turn the dough out on to a floured surface and flatten it out into a circle. Grease a 26 cm (10½ inch) loose-bottomed flan tin. Fit the dough into the tin so the dough comes slightly up the sides.

Peel, core and slice the apples and toss them with the lemon juice and the remaining 2 tablespoons sugar. Arrange the slices over the dough and scatter with the blackberries. Spoon the crumble mixture over the top and bake in a preheated oven, 200°C (400°F), Gas Mark 6, for 50–60 minutes until cooked through (test by piercing the cake in the centre to check that the dough is cooked). Cover with foil during cooking if the topping starts to over-brown.

For crumbly plum & ginger torte, make the dough as above, adding 2 pieces chopped stem ginger instead of the mixed spice. Break 100 g (3½ oz) gingernut biscuits into a food processor. Add 50 g (2 oz) unsalted butter and 4 tablespoons light muscovado sugar. Blend until the mixture has a coarse, crumble consistency. Once the dough is in the tin, scatter with 450 g (14½ oz) stoned and sliced plums. Spoon the gingernut mixture over the top and bake as above.

date, sultana & hazelnut bread

Makes **1 large loaf**
Time **1–2 hours**, depending
  on machine

275 ml (9 fl oz) **warm water**
2 tablespoons **sunflower oil**
1 teaspoon **salt**
2 tablespoons **milk powder**
25 g (1 oz) **toasted
  wheatgerm**
200 g (7 oz) **strong
  wholemeal flour**
200 g (7 oz) **strong white
  bread flour**
2 tablespoons **dark
  muscovado sugar**
2¾ teaspoons **fast-action
  dried yeast**
50 g (2 oz) **hazelnuts**,
  toasted and roughly
  chopped
100 g (3½ oz) **pitted dates**,
  sliced
75 g (3 oz) **sultanas**

Lift the bread pan out of the machine and fit the blade. Put the ingredients in the pan, following the order specified in the manual. Add the hazelnuts, dates and sultanas with the flour.

Fit the pan into the machine and close the lid. Set to a 750 g (1½ lb) loaf size on a fast/rapid bake setting.

At the end of the programme lift the pan out of the machine and shake the bread out on to a wire rack to cool.

For fast-baked almond & amaretti bread, roughly chop 100 g (3½ oz) unblanched almonds. Put 100 g (3½ oz) amaretti biscuits in a polythene bag and crush with a rolling pin. Put 175 ml (6 fl oz) warm milk, 200 g (7 oz) Greek yogurt, 50 g (2 oz) soft butter, ½ teaspoon salt, 400 g (13 oz) strong white bread flour, 25 g (1 oz) light muscovado sugar and 2½ teaspoons fast-action dried yeast in the bread pan. Add the almonds and crushed biscuits with the flour. Set to a 750 g (1½ lb) loaf size on the fast/rapid bake programme. After baking, dust with icing sugar.

cherry & frangipane twist

Makes **1 large loaf**
Time **1½–2½ hours**,
    depending on machine, plus
    shaping, proving and baking

Dough

250 ml (8 fl oz) **water**

1 **egg**, beaten

2 tablespoons **butter**, at room
    temperature

½ teaspoon **salt**

2 tablespoons **milk powder**

500 g (1 lb) **strong white
    bread flour**

1 tablespoon **caster sugar**

1¼ teaspoons **fast-action
    dried yeast**

Filling

100 g (3½ oz) **butter**, at room
    temperature

100 g (3½ oz) **caster sugar**

1 **egg**, beaten

100 g (3½ oz) **ground almonds**

½ teaspoon **almond essence**

425 g (14 oz) can **black
    cherries**, drained

To finish

3 tablespoons **milk**

3 tablespoons **flaked almonds**

3 tablespoons **icing sugar**

Lift the bread pan out of the machine and fit the blade. Put the dough ingredients in the pan, following the order specified in the manual. Fit the pan into the machine and close the lid. Set to the dough programme.

Meanwhile, make the frangipane filling by creaming together the butter and sugar. Add the egg, almonds and almond essence and mix together.

At the end of the programme turn the dough out on to a floured surface and roll it out to a rectangle, 38 x 30 cm (15 x 12 inches).

Spread the frangipane over the dough to within about 2 cm (¾ inches) of the edge. Sprinkle the cherries over the top, then roll up the dough, starting from one of the longer edges. Twist the rolled-up dough to give a corkscrew effect then carefully transfer it to a greased baking tray. Cover with oiled clingfilm and leave in a warm place for about 30–40 minutes or until well risen.

Brush with milk, sprinkle with the flaked almonds and bake in a preheated oven, 200°C (400°F), Gas Mark 6, for about 25 minutes until golden and the bread sounds hollow when tapped with the fingertips. Cover with foil after 15 minutes if over-browning. Transfer to a wire rack and dust with sifted icing sugar. Serve warm or cold.

For apricot frangipane twist, add the crushed seeds of 10 cardamom pods to the frangipane paste and finish as above. Use 350 g (11½ oz) sliced fresh apricots instead of the cherries.

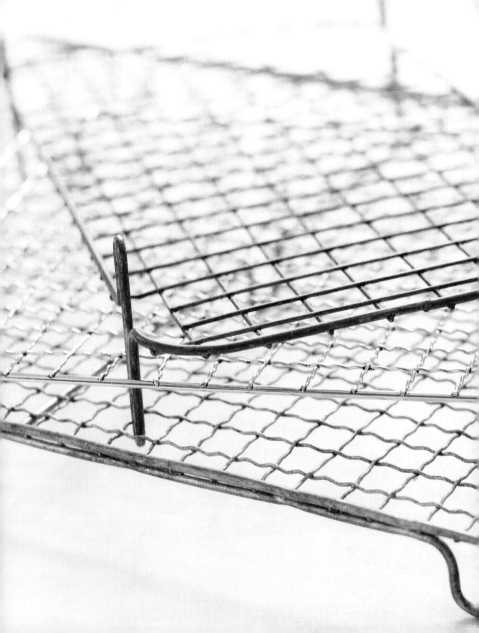

cakes

cherry & almond madeira cake

Makes **8 slices**

Time about 1¼ **hours**,
depending on machine, plus
cooking

75 g (3 oz) **dried black
cherries**

75 ml (3 fl oz) **apple juice**

175 g (6 oz) **unsalted butter**,
softened

175 g (6 oz) **caster sugar**,
plus extra for dusting

3 large **eggs**, beaten

225 g (7½ oz) **self-raising
flour**

½ teaspoon **baking powder**

100 g (3½ oz) **ground
almonds**

1 teaspoon **almond extract**

Put the cherries and apple juice in a small saucepan
and heat gently, uncovered, for about 5 minutes until
the cherries have plumped up slightly and the juice has
been absorbed. Leave to cool.

Lift the bread pan out of the machine and fit the blade.
Put the ingredients, except the cherries, in the pan,
following the order specified in the manual.

Fit the pan into the machine and close the lid. Set to
the cake programme. After about 5 minutes use a
plastic spatula to scrape the mixture down from the
sides and from the corners of the pan. Scatter the
cherries into the pan once the cake is evenly mixed.

Test the cake after 1¼ hours by inserting a skewer into
the centre. If it comes out clean the cake is ready. If
not, cook a little longer or complete the programme.

Transfer the cake to a wire rack to cool. Serve dusted
with extra sugar.

For coffee & walnut madeira cake, omit the cherries,
juice and almond extract. Dissolve 1 tablespoon
espresso coffee powder in 2 tablespoons boiling
water and add to the pan with the remaining
ingredients. Make as above, adding 100 g (3½ oz)
roughly chopped walnuts to the pan once the cake is
evenly mixed. Finish as above.

sticky marmalade cake

Makes **8 slices**
Time about 1¼ **hours**,
  depending on machine

125 g (4 oz) **hazelnuts**
100 g (3½ oz) coarse or fine-
  shred **citrus marmalade**,
  plus 4 tablespoons
100 g (3½ oz) **stem ginger**
  from a jar, finely chopped
175 g (6 oz) **unsalted butter**,
  softened
75 g (3 oz) **light muscovado
  sugar**
3 **eggs**, beaten
225 g (7½ oz) **self-raising flour**
1 teaspoon **baking powder**

Grind 75 g (3 oz) hazelnuts in a food processor.
Roughly chop the remainder.

Lift the bread pan out of the machine and fit the blade.
Put the ingredients, except the 4 tablespoons
marmalade, in the pan, following the order specified in
the manual.

Fit the pan into the machine and close the lid. Set to
the cake programme. After about 5 minutes use a
plastic spatula to scrape the mixture down from the
sides and from the corners of the pan.

Test the cake after 1¼ hours by inserting a skewer into
the centre. If it comes out clean the cake is ready. If
not, cook a little longer or complete the programme.

Transfer the cake to a wire rack. Melt the extra
4 tablespoons marmalade in a small saucepan with
1 tablespoon water. (Sieve the marmalade to remove
the shreds first, if liked.) Brush over the cake and leave
to cool.

For citrus cream cheese cake, make the cake as
above then beat 200 g (7 oz) cream cheese in a bowl
with the finely grated rind of 1 orange and 200 g
(7 oz) icing sugar until smooth. Use a palette knife to
spread the frosting over the top and sides of the cake.

moist & fruity teacake

Makes **8–10 slices**

Time about **50 minutes**,
depending on machine,
plus standing

225 g (7½ oz) luxury **mixed
dried fruit**

150 g (5 oz) **light muscovado
sugar**, plus a little extra for
sprinkling

4 tablespoons **malt extract**

125 g (4 oz) **shredded bran
or bran-flake cereal**

1½ teaspoons **ground mixed
spice**

350 ml (12 fl oz) **milk**

200 g (7 oz) **self-raising flour**

1 teaspoon **baking powder**

Lift the bread pan out of the machine and fit the blade. Add the dried fruit, sugar, malt extract, cereal, spice and milk to the pan. Stir gently to mix, then leave to stand for 20 minutes.

Add the flour and baking powder, fit the pan into the machine and close the lid. Set to the cake programme. After about 5 minutes use a plastic spatula to scrape the mixture down from the sides and from the corners of the pan.

Test the cake after 50 minutes by inserting a skewer into the centre. If it comes out clean the cake is ready. If not, cook a little longer or complete the programme.

Transfer the cake to a wire rack and sprinkle with extra sugar. Leave to cool. Serve sliced and buttered.

For date & pecan teacake, lightly toast 100 g (3½ oz) pecans and roughly chop them along with 125 g (4 oz) pitted dates. Put in the bread pan with the sugar, cereal, spice and milk as above and using date syrup instead of the malt extract. Leave to cool as above before completing.

chocolate fudge slice

Makes **10 slices**

Time about **1 hour**, depending on machine

Cake

75 g (3 oz) **cocoa powder**

75 g (3 oz) **plain dark chocolate**, chopped

150 g (5 oz) **unsalted butter**, softened

250 g (8 oz) **light muscovado sugar**

2 large **eggs**, beaten

200 g (7 oz) **self-raising flour**

½ teaspoon **baking powder**

Icing

200 g (7 oz) **plain dark chocolate**

175 g (6 oz) **golden icing sugar**

150 g (5 oz) **unsalted butter**, softened

Whisk the cocoa powder in a bowl with 225 ml (7½ fl oz) boiling water until smooth. Stir in the chopped chocolate and leave to cool, stirring occasionally, until the chocolate has melted.

Lift the bread pan out of the machine and fit the blade. Put the cake ingredients in the pan.

Fit the pan into the machine and close the lid. Set to the cake programme. After about 5 minutes use a plastic spatula to scrape the mixture down from the sides and from the corners of the pan.

Test the cake after 1 hour by inserting a skewer into the centre. If it comes out clean the cake is ready. If not, cook a little longer or complete the programme. Transfer the cake to a wire rack to cool.

Make the icing. Melt the chocolate in a small bowl and leave to cool slightly. Beat together the icing sugar and butter, then beat in the chocolate. Split the cake in half and sandwich with one quarter of the icing. Transfer to a serving plate and use a palette knife to spread the remaining icing over the top and sides.

For double chocolate fudge slice, make the cake as above, then measure 250 ml (8 fl oz) double cream and pour half into a small saucepan. Heat gently until it bubbles around the edges, then remove from the heat and tip in 250 g (8 oz) chopped white chocolate. Leave to stand for a few minutes until the chocolate has melted, then stir lightly and turn into a bowl. Leave until cool. Add the remaining cream and whisk with a hand-held electric whisk until the mixture just starts to hold its shape. Use to cover the cake.

spicy apple parkin

Makes **8 slices**

Time about **1 hour**, depending on machine, plus cooking

4 tart **dessert apples**, such as Granny Smith

5 tablespoons **apple juice**

¼ teaspoon **ground cloves**

175 g (6 oz) **black treacle**

150 g (5 oz) **golden syrup**

75 g (3 oz) **unsalted butter**, softened

100 g (3½ oz) **self-raising wholemeal flour**

100 g (3½ oz) **self-raising white flour**

1 teaspoon **bicarbonate of soda**

2 teaspoons **ground ginger**

175 g (6 oz) medium **oatmeal**

Peel, core and slice the apples and put the slices in a small saucepan with the apple juice and ground cloves. Bring to the boil, reduce the heat and cook gently, uncovered, for about 5 minutes or until the apples have softened slightly. Drain and leave to cool.

Lift the bread pan out of the machine and fit the blade. Add the treacle, syrup, butter, flour, bicarbonate of soda, ginger and oatmeal to the pan.

Fit the pan into the machine and close the lid. Set to the cake programme. After about 5 minutes use a plastic spatula to scrape the mixture down from the sides and from the corners of the pan. Stir in the apples.

Test the cake after 1 hour by inserting a skewer into the centre. If it comes out clean the cake is ready. If not, cook a little longer or complete the programme. Transfer the cake to a wire rack to cool.

For brandied prune parkin, roughly chop 200 g (7 oz) prunes. Make the cake mixture as above, omitting the first step and adding the prunes, 2 tablespoons brandy and the grated rind of 1 orange with the rest of the ingredients.

tropical fruit drizzle cake

Makes **8–10 slices**
Time about **1¼ hours**,
   depending on machine

125 g (4 oz) **semi-dried
   tropical fruits**, such as
   mango, papaya and
   pineapple
100 g (3½ oz) **creamed
   coconut**
150 g (5 oz) **unsalted butter**,
   softened
175 g (6 oz) **golden caster
   sugar**
3 **eggs**, beaten
finely grated rind of 3 **limes**,
   plus 4 tablespoons juice
225 g (7½ oz) **self-raising
   flour**
1 teaspoon **baking powder**
4 tablespoons **caster sugar,**
   for sprinkling

Roughly chop the tropical fruit mix if it is in large pieces. If the creamed coconut is in a solid block microwave on medium power for 2–3 minutes to make a soft paste.

Lift the bread pan out of the machine and fit the blade. Add half the chopped fruits, the creamed coconut, butter, 175 g (6 oz) caster sugar, eggs, lime rind, flour and baking powder to the pan.

Fit the pan into the machine and close the lid. Set to the cake programme. After about 5 minutes use a plastic spatula to scrape the mixture down from the sides and from the corners of the pan. Scatter in the remaining tropical fruit mixture.

Test the cake after 1¼ hours by inserting a skewer into the centre. If it comes out clean the cake is ready. If not, cook a little longer or complete the programme. Transfer the cake to a wire rack to cool.

While the cake is still warm, drizzle over the lime juice and then sprinkle over the sugar. Leave to cool.

For lemon & coconut drizzle cake, omit the tropical fruits and use the rind of 3 lemons instead of the lime, and use ordinary caster sugar instead of golden caster sugar. While the cake is cooking blend 4 tablespoons lemon juice with 4 tablespoons caster sugar. Transfer the cake to a wire rack and drizzle over the lemon syrup.

cheat's stollen

Makes **1 large loaf**
Time **2¾–3½ hours**, depending
on machine

Dough
1 **egg**, beaten
175 ml (6 fl oz) **milk**
50 g (2 oz) **butter**, melted
½ teaspoon **salt**
grated rind of 1 **lemon**
½ teaspoon **nutmeg**, grated
4 **cardamom pods**, seeds
   crushed and pods discarded
375 g (12 oz) **strong white**
   bread flour
50 g (2 oz) **caster sugar**
1¼ teaspoons **fast-action**
   dried yeast
75 g (3 oz) **mixed dried fruit**
50 g (2 oz) **glacé cherries**,
   roughly chopped
75 g (3 oz) yellow **marzipan**,
   diced

To finish
1 tablespoon **butter**
2 tablespoons **icing sugar**, for
   dusting

Lift the bread pan out of the machine and fit the blade. Put the dough ingredients, except the dried fruit and marzipan, in the pan, following the order specified in the manual.

Fit the pan into the machine and close the lid. Set to a 750 g (1½ lb) loaf size on the sweet programme.

Add the dried fruit and marzipan when the machine beeps, adding them in small batches so that the blade does not get jammed.

At the end of the programme lift the pan out of the machine and shake the bread out on to a wire rack. Rub the top with the butter and dust heavily with sifted icing sugar. Leave to cool.

For mini stollen bites, make as above but set to the dough programme, adding the fruit and marzipan when the machine beeps. Turn out the dough on to a floured surface and roll to fit a greased 28 x 18 cm (11 X 7 inch) shallow baking tin. Lift into the tin, pressing the dough into the corners. Cover loosely with oiled clingfilm and leave until risen by half its size. Bake in a preheated oven, 200°C (400°F), Gas Mark 6, for 20–25 minutes until golden. Cool on a wire rack. Serve cut in squares, generously dusted with icing sugar.

gluten-free breads

chickpea loaf with crushed spices

Makes **1 large loaf**
Time **1–2 hours**, depending
on machine

200 g (7 oz) cooked
chickpeas
350 ml (12 fl oz) warm **water**
2 **eggs**, beaten
4 tablespoons **olive oil**
1½ teaspoons **salt**
finely grated rind of 1 **lemon**
1 teaspoon **ground turmeric**
2 teaspoons **coriander seeds**,
crushed
2 teaspoons **cumin seeds**,
crushed
15 g (½ oz) **coriander leaves**,
chopped
400 g (13 oz) **wheat- and
gluten-free bread flour**
2 teaspoons **caster sugar**
2 teaspoons **fast-action dried
yeast**

Crush the chickpeas, either in a food processor or by mashing them in a bowl with a fork.

Lift the bread pan out of the machine and fit the blade. Put the ingredients in the pan, following the order specified for gluten-free breads in the manual. The chickpeas should be added with the liquids.

Fit the pan into the machine and close the lid. Set to a 750 g (1½ lb) loaf size on the fast/rapid bake programme.

At the end of the programme lift the pan out of the machine and shake the bread out on to a wire rack to cool.

For chilli & herb butter, to spread on the bread, beat 125 g (4 oz) softened butter in a bowl. Add 1 deseeded and finely chopped mild chilli, 3 tablespoons snipped chives, 2 tablespoons finely chopped parsley, 1 tablespoon chopped mint and a little salt. Beat well until evenly mixed, then turn into a small dish. Cover and chill until ready to serve.

simple gluten-free white bread

Makes 1 large loaf
Time 1–2 hours, depending
on machine

Dough
2 **eggs**, beaten
375 ml (12 fl oz) warm **milk**
1 teaspoon **lemon juice**
25 g (1 oz) **unsalted butter**,
softened
1½ teaspoons **salt**
400 g (13 oz) **gluten-free
white bread flour**
100 g (3½ oz) **rice flour or
quinoa flour**
1 tablespoon **caster sugar**
2 teaspoons **fast-action dried
yeast**

To finish
melted **butter**, to brush
sesame seeds or **poppy
seeds**, for sprinkling

Lift the bread pan out of the machine and fit the blade.
Put the dough ingredients in the pan, following the
order specified for gluten-free breads in the manual.

Fit the pan into the machine and close the lid. Set
to a 750 g (1½ lb) loaf size on the fast/rapid bake
programme.

At the end of the programme lift the pan out of the
machine and shake the bread out on to a wire rack.
Brush the top with butter and sprinkle with sesame or
poppy seeds.

For seeded gluten-free white bread, lightly toast
3 tablespoons sesame seeds in a dry frying pan until
lightly toasted. Add to the bread pan with the flour
and 2 tablespoons each of linseeds, sunflower seeds
and pumpkin seeds. After removing the bread from the
pan, brush with butter and sprinkle with extra seeds.

roasted red pepper cornbread

Makes **1 large loaf**

Time **1–2 hours**, depending
on machine, plus cooking

1 **red pepper**, cored,
deseeded and quartered

1 tablespoon **olive oil**

2 **eggs**, beaten

350 ml (12 fl oz) **milk**, warmed

50 g (2 oz) **unsalted butter**,
melted

1 teaspoon **salt**

50 g (2 oz) **Parmesan
cheese**, grated

1 large, mild **red chilli**,
deseeded and finely chopped

1 teaspoon **white wine
vinegar** or **malt vinegar**

125 g (4 oz) fine **ground corn**
(masa harina)

300 g (10 oz) **wheat- and
gluten-free bread flour** with
added natural gum

2 teaspoons **caster sugar**

2 teaspoons **fast-action dried
yeast**

4 **spring onions**, chopped

melted **butter**, to brush

Put the pepper quarters, skin side up, on the grill rack,
brush with oil and grill for 10 minutes until the skins
are blackened. Wrap in foil, leave to cool, then peel off
the skins and roughly chop the flesh.

Lift the bread pan out of the machine and fit the blade.
Put the ingredients in the pan, following the order
specified for gluten-free breads in the manual. Add
the chopped peppers and spring onions with the sugar
and yeast.

Fit the pan into the machine and close the lid. Set to a
750 g (1½ lb) loaf size on a fast/rapid bake programme.

At the end of the programme lift the pan out of the
machine and shake the bread out on to a wire rack.
Brush the top with the butter and brown under the grill,
if liked. Leave to cool.

glazed pear & cinnamon loaf

Makes **1 large loaf**

Time **1–2 hours**, depending on machine, plus soaking

100 g (3½ oz) **dried pears**, chopped

100 g (3½ oz) **sultanas**

400 ml (14 fl oz) strong, hot **tea**

1 **egg**, beaten

25 g (1 oz) **unsalted butter**, softened

¼ teaspoon **salt**

2 teaspoons **ground cinnamon**

375 g (12 oz) **gluten-free white bread flour**

75 g (3 oz) **light muscovado sugar**

1½ teaspoons **fast-action dried yeast**

icing sugar, for dusting

Put the chopped pears and sultanas in a bowl with the hot tea and leave to soak for 1 hour.

Lift the bread pan out of the machine and fit the blade. Put the ingredients in the pan, following the order specified for gluten-free breads in the manual. Add the sultanas with the pears and liquid.

Fit the pan into the machine and close the lid. Set to a 750 g (1½ lb) loaf size on the fast/rapid bake programme.

At the end of the programme lift the pan out of the machine and shake the bread out on to a wire rack. Serve freshly baked or toasted and buttered.

For white chocolate & ginger loaf, omit the pears and increase the sultanas to 200 g (7 oz), soaking them in 400 ml (14 fl oz) strong hot tea. Chop 150 g (5 oz) white chocolate into pieces. Continue as above, substituting 25 g (1 oz) of the gluten-free flour with cocoa powder and adding the chopped chocolate when the machine beeps.

sunflower, yogurt & apricot bread

Makes **1 large loaf**
Time **1–2 hours**, depending
on machine

250 ml (8 fl oz) warm **water**
2 **eggs**, beaten
4 tablespoons **sunflower oil**
150 ml (5 fl oz) **Greek yogurt**,
plus extra to serve (optional)
1 teaspoon **salt**
475 g (15 oz) **wheat- and
gluten-free bread flour** with
added natural gum
2 tablespoons **light
muscovado sugar**
2 teaspoons **fast-action dried
yeast**
50 g (2 oz) **sunflower seeds**
125 g (4 oz) ready-to-eat
dried apricots, diced
icing sugar, for dusting

Lift the bread pan out of the machine and fit the blade.
Put the ingredients in the pan, following the order
specified for gluten-free breads in the manual. Add the
seeds and apricots with the sugar and yeast.

Fit the pan into the machine and close the lid. Set to a
750 g (1½ lb) loaf size on fast/rapid bake programme.

At the end of the programme lift the pan out of the
machine and shake the bread out on to a wire rack.
Dust with icing sugar, then grill until browned. Leave to
cool. Serve with more greek yogurt, blueberries and
honey (if liked).

For breakfast loaf with tropical fruits, chop 175 g
(6 oz) semi-dried tropical fruits (such as mango,
papaya and pineapple) into small pieces. Make the
bread as above, using the chopped fruits instead of
the apricots and sunflower seeds and using 150 ml
(5 fl oz) tropical fruit-flavoured yogurt instead of the
Greek yogurt.

sun-dried tomato & herb bread

Makes **1 large loaf**
Time **1–2 hours**, depending
on machine, plus soaking

75 g (3 oz) **buckwheat**
250 ml (8 fl oz) warm **water**
2 **eggs**, beaten
75 g (3 oz) **sun-dried tomato
paste**
25 g (1 oz) **unsalted butter**,
softened
1 teaspoon **celery salt**
300 g (10 oz) **gluten-free
bread flour**
2 teaspoons **caster sugar**
2 teaspoons **fast-action dried
yeast**
small handful of chopped
fresh herbs, such as
parsley, chervil, rosemary,
chives and oregano
50 g (2 oz) **sun-dried
tomatoes** in olive oil,
drained and sliced

Put the buckwheat in a bowl and add 100 ml (3½ fl oz) boiling water. Leave to soak for 20 minutes until the water has been absorbed.

Lift the bread pan out of the machine and fit the blade. Put the buckwheat in the pan with all the ingredients, except the herbs and sliced sun-dried tomatoes, following the order specified for gluten-free breads in the manual.

Fit the pan into the machine and close the lid. Set to a 750 g (1½ lb) loaf size on a fast/rapid bake programme. Add the herbs and sliced sun-dried tomatoes when the machine beeps.

At the end of the programme lift the pan out of the machine and shake the bread out on to a wire rack to cool.

For pesto & pine nut bread, toast 75 g (3 oz) pine nuts in a dry frying pan and leave to cool. Finely chop 1 tablespoon rosemary. Soak the buckwheat in the water as above and put it in the machine with 2 eggs, 250 ml (8 fl oz) warm water, 75 g (3 oz) green pesto, 25 g (1 oz) very soft butter, 1 teaspoon celery salt, 1 teaspoon freshly ground black pepper, the pine nuts, rosemary, 300 g (10 oz) gluten-free bread flour, 2 teaspoons caster sugar and 2 teaspoons fast-action dried yeast. Continue as above.

roasted vegetable loaf with wild rice

Makes **1 small loaf**
Time **1¾–2 hours**, depending
on machine, plus cooking

150 g (5 oz) **mixed roasted
  vegetables**, drained if
  packed in a jar with oil, or
  homemade (see below)
50 g (2 oz) **wild rice**
3 tablespoons **olive oil**
2 **eggs**, beaten
250 ml (8 fl oz) **milk**
200 g (7 oz) **cornmeal** or
  polenta
150 g (5 oz) **rice flour**
1 teaspoon **salt**
1 tablespoon **wheat-free
  baking powder**
1 teaspoon hot **paprika**, plus
  extra for sprinkling

Roughly chop the vegetables if they are in large
pieces. Cook the rice in boiling water for about 20
minutes until just tender. Drain and leave to cool.

Lift the bread pan out of the machine and fit the blade.
Put the ingredients, except the roasted vegetables, in
the pan, following the order specified in the manual.

Fit the pan into the machine and close the lid. Set to
the cake programme. After about 5 minutes use a
plastic spatula to scrape the mixture down from the
sides and from the corners of the pan. Scatter in the
vegetables and a sprinkling of extra paprika once the
loaf is evenly mixed.

Test the loaf after 1¾ hours by inserting a skewer into
the centre. If it comes out clean the loaf is ready. If not,
cook a little longer or complete the programme.

At the end of the programme lift the pan out of the
machine and shake the loaf out on to a wire rack
to cool. Serve warm, buttered, if liked.

For homemade roasted vegetables, deseed 3 mixed
peppers and cut them into chunks. Scatter in a
roasting tin with 2 thinly sliced courgettes and 1 small
red onion cut into wedges. Drizzle with 2 tablespoons
olive oil and sprinkle with 1 teaspoon chopped thyme
and 1 teaspoon crushed fennel or coriander seeds.
Roast in a preheated oven, 200°C (400°F), Gas Mark
6, for 50–60 minutes until tender and beginning to
brown. Leave to cool and refrigerate for up to 3 days.

herb bread

Makes **1 large loaf**
Time about **1–2 hours**,
   depending on machine,
   plus cooking

150 g (5 oz) **parsnips**
400 ml (14 fl oz) warm **water**
2 tablespoons **olive oil**
1 teaspoon **salt**
200 g (7 oz) **chickpea flour**
300 g (10 oz) **gluten-free
   bread flour**
4 tablespoons chopped
   mixed herbs
1 teaspoon **caster sugar**
2½ teaspoons **fast-action
   dried yeast**

Peel and dice the parsnips. Cook them in a saucepan of boiling water for 10 minutes, then drain and mash.

Lift the bread pan out of the machine and fit the blade. Put the ingredients in the pan, following the order specified for gluten-free breads in the manual. Add the mashed parsnip with the water.

Fit the pan into the machine and close the lid. Set to a 750 g (1½ lb) loaf size on the fast/rapid bake programme.

At the end of the programme lift the pan out of the machine and shake the bread out on to a wire rack to cool. If the bread looks pale when you take it out of the machine, brush the top with a little melted butter or oil and grill for a few minutes until browned.

For spiced potato loaf, use the same quantity of mashed potato to replace the parsnip. Crush 2 teaspoons each of cumin and coriander seeds using a pestle and mortar and mix with ½ teaspoon crushed dried chillies. Add to the pan instead of the mixed herbs and replace the salt with celery salt. Continue as above.

chilli corn bread

Makes **1 large loaf**

Time about **1¾–2 hours**,
  depending on machine

2 **eggs**, beaten

150 ml (5 fl oz) **natural yogurt**

300 ml (½ pint) **milk**

50 g (2 oz) **unsalted butter**,
  softened

50 g (2 oz) **Parmesan
  cheese**, grated

1 tablespoon **caster sugar**

150 g (5 oz) **yellow cornmeal**

250 g (8 oz) **plain flour**

3 teaspoons **baking powder**

1 teaspoon **bicarbonate of
  soda**

1 teaspoon **salt**

black pepper

2 large whole **dried chillies**,
  finely chopped

6 **spring onions**, finely
  chopped

Lift the bread pan out of the machine and fit the blade. Put the ingredients, except the chillies and onions, in the pan, following the order specified for gluten-free breads in the manual.

Fit the pan into the machine and close the lid. Set to the cake programme. After about 5 minutes use a plastic spatula to scrape the mixture down from the sides and from the corners of the pan. Add the chillies and onion.

Test the bread 15 minutes before the end of the programme by inserting a skewer into the centre. If it comes out cleanly, the bread is ready. If not, leave until the programme ends and then retest.

Lift the pan out of the machine and shake the bread out on to a wire rack to cool. Serve with bowls of chilli, if liked.

For five spice corn bread, omit the chillies from the recipe above and use a finely chopped red onion instead of the spring onions. Crush together using a pestle and mortar, 1 teaspoon crushed dried chillies, 2 teaspoons cumin seeds, 2 teaspoons coriander seeds, 1 teaspoon black mustard seeds and 1 teaspoon celery seeds. Tip into a dry frying pan and heat for a couple of minutes to lightly toast the seeds. Add to the bread pan with the flour.

index

almonds: cherry & almond madeira cake 202
fast-baked almond & amaretti bread 196
homemade marzipan 184
sour cherry & almond rings 134
amaretti biscuits: fast baked almond & amaretti bread 196
apples: apple & ginger coils 142
crumbly blackberry & apple torte 194
pecan & apple rings 134
spicy apple parkin 210
apricots: apricot frangipane twist 198
buckwheat, linseed & apricot bread 46
sunflower, yogurt & apricot bread 226
artichokes: artichoke & Gruyère stromboli 50
pancetta & artichoke pizza 80
Asian-style flatbreads 108
asparagus & tarragon buns 132

bacon: fennel, bacon & Gruyère twist 58
spicy potato bread 82
baharat spice blend 110
bananas: seeded banana loaf 178
white chocolate & banana loaf 170
baps, floury 138

barley: date & malted barley bread 42
basil: buttered garlic & basil sticks 100
cherry tomato & basil buns 132
beans: goats' cheese & bean mini loaves 124
beer & brown sugar bread 64
berry bread with orange liqueur 174
black bread, Irish 68
blackberry & apple torte 194
blueberries: blueberry & vanilla plait 164
blueberry conserve 36
Boston brown bread 34
brandied prune & chocolate slice 176
brandied prune parkin 210
bread sticks: grissini 116
grissini with aromatic salt 116
Parmesan & olive 104
bread-making machines 8, 11–14
breakfast loaf with tropical fruits 226
breakfast muesli bread 36
brioche 40
baby chocolate brioche buns 40
broad beans: chorizo & broad bean tostadas 96
goats' cheese & bean mini loaves 124
buckwheat flour: buckwheat, linseed & apricot bread 46
buns: apple & ginger coils 142
asparagus & tarragon buns 132
baby chocolate brioche buns 40
cherry tomato & basil buns 132

chocolate, fruit & nut buns 172
chorizo & Manchego buns 122
Devonshire splits 140
hot cross buns 156
iced finger buns 118
lemon splits 140
pecan & apple rings 134
prosciutto & Parmesan crown 122
sour cherry & almond rings 134
sticky Chelsea buns 172
butter 10
chilli & herb butter 218
honey butter 148
maple butter 166
spiced rum butter 182
buttered garlic & basil sticks 100
buttermilk: oatmeal & buttermilk bread 20

Cajun spices, seeded pumpkin bread with 84
cakes 200–13
brandied prune parkin 210
cheat's stollen 214
cherry & almond madeira cake 202
chocolate fudge slice 208
coffee & walnut madeira cake 202
crumbly plum & ginger cake 194
date & pecan teacake 206
lemon & coconut drizzle cake 212
moist & fruity teacake 206
spiced peach & redcurrant cake 188
spicy apple parkin 210
sticky marmalade cake 204

tropical fruit drizzle cake 212
white chocolate & pecan cake 190
caraway seeds: fast baked rye & caraway bread 38
cardamom: pine nut, lemon & cardamom loaf 180
carrots: wholemeal carrot & onion loaves 130
challah 152
cheat's stollen 214
Cheddar cheese & chutney ring 76
cheese: artichoke & Gruyère stromboli 50
Cheddar cheese & chutney ring 76
chorizo & Manchego buns 122
Emmenthal & hot pepper bread 88
fennel, bacon & Gruyère twist 58
feta & onion pide 102
feta & yogurt dip 74
feta, mint & cucumber rolls 124
Italian wraps with mozzarella & cured meats 98
leek & Stilton picnic slice 78
mushroom & mozzarella stromboli 50
onion & red Leicester bread 86
onion, sage & Gorgonzola focaccia 94
pancetta & Parmesan bread 70
Parmesan & olive bread sticks 104
potted cheese 64
prosciutto & Parmesan crown 122
seeded cheese batons 32

spinach & Manchego ring loaf 76
Stilton & spinach whirl 86
see also cream cheese; goats' cheese
cheesecake slice, summer fruit 188
Chelsea buns, sticky 172
cherries: cherry & almond madeira cake 202
cherry & frangipane twist 198
sour cherry & almond rings 134
cherry tomato & basil buns 132
chicken: spicy chicken mole with chilli bread 60
spicy chicken wraps 108
chickpea flour: spiced chickpea flatbreads 110
spicy chickpea & onion loaf 56
chickpeas: chickpea loaf with crushed spices 218
chillies: chilli & herb butter 218
chilli & smoked paprika bread 54
chilli chocolate bread 60
chilli corn bread 234
Emmenthal & hot pepper bread 88
spicy chicken mole with chilli bread 60
spicy peanut & chilli loaf 54
chocolate: baby chocolate brioche buns 40
brandied prune & chocolate slice 176
chilli chocolate bread 60
chocolate & pecan spiral 176
chocolate, fruit & nut buns 172

chocolate fudge slice 208
dark chocolate & ginger rolls 170
doughnuts with chocolate sauce 114
gooey chocolate nut bread 190
white chocolate & banana loaf 170
white chocolate & ginger slice 224
white chocolate & pecan cake 190
white chocolate cream frosting 208
chorizo: chorizo & broad bean tostadas 96
chorizo & Manchego buns 122
chunky fruit & nut loaf 168
chutney: Cheddar cheese & chutney ring 76
ciabatta 26
sun-dried tomato & herb ciabatta 26
ciambella mandorlata 146
cinnamon: cinnamon doughnuts 114
glazed pear & cinnamon loaf 224
pear, cinnamon & raisin kügelhopf 186
citrus cream cheese frosting 204
clementine & fig savarins 136
coconut: lemon & coconut drizzle cake 212
tropical fruit drizzle cake 212
coffee: coffee & walnut bread 166
coffee & walnut madeira cake 202
conserve, fresh blueberry 36
coriander: cumin & coriander sticks 100

cornmeal: chilli corn bread 234
five spice corn bread 234
roasted red pepper cornbread 222
cottage loaf, seeded 18
courgettes: minted courgette & lemon loaf 74
couronne 28
cranberry & pomegranate bread 46
cream cheese: citrus cream cheese frosting 204
crumbly blackberry & apple torte 194
crumbly plum & ginger cake 194
crust, colour 13
cucumber: feta, mint & cucumber rolls 124
cumin & coriander sticks 100

dates: date & malted barley bread 42
date & pecan teacake 206
date, sultana & hazelnut bread 196
sticky toffee & date loaf 162
Devonshire splits 140
dill: sweet dill & mustard loaf 52
dinner rolls 126
dip, feta & yogurt 74
doughnuts: cinnamon doughnuts 114
with chocolate sauce 114

Easter wreath, Greek 148
easy sourdough bread 28
Emmenthal & hot pepper bread 88
enriched poppy seed & lemon loaf 152
enriching ingredients 10
equipment 8

fennel seeds: fennel, bacon & Gruyère twist 58
yogurt, honey & fennel seed bread 44
feta & onion pide 102
feta & yogurt dip 74
feta, mint & cucumber rolls 124
figs: clementine & fig savarins 136
poppy seed, orange & fig loaf 178
finger buns, iced 118
five spice corn bread 234
flat breads 90–111
flatbreads, Asian-style 108
florentine loaf, orange 180
flours 9
focaccia: onion, sage & Gorgonzola 94
tomato 94
fougasse 104
frangipane: apricot frangipane twist 198
cherry & frangipane twist 198
French toast with yogurt, strawberries & honey 20
frosting: citrus cream cheese 204
white chocolate cream 208
fruited Boston bread 34
fruited teacakes 118

garlic: buttered garlic & basil sticks 100
garlic & rosemary twigs 120
ginger: apple & ginger coils 142
crumbly plum & ginger cake 194
dark chocolate & ginger rolls 170
lardy cake with ginger 192
pear & ginger loaf with lemon glaze 160

white chocolate & ginger slice 224
gluten-free breads 216–35
gluten-free flours 9
goats' cheese: goats' cheese & bean mini loaves 124
goats' cheese & onion pizzas 80
gooey chocolate nut bread 190
granary bread 22
Greek Easter wreath 148
grissini 116
with aromatic salt 116

hazelnuts: date, sultana & hazelnut bread 196
hazelnut marzipan 150
herb bread 232
herbs 10–11
honey: French toast with yogurt, strawberries & honey 20
honey butter 148
walnut & honey bread 30
yogurt, honey & fennel seed bread 44
hot cross bun loaf 156
hot cross buns 156

iced finger buns 118
ingredients 8–11, 14
Irish black bread 68
Italian wraps with mozzarella & cured meats 98

jam: Devonshire splits 140

knots, sesame 128
küchen, nectarine & marzipan fruit 184
kügelhopf: pear, cinnamon & raisin 186
spiced plum 186

lardy cake 192
lardy cake with ginger 192
leek & Stilton picnic slice 78
lemon: enriched poppy seed & lemon loaf 152
lemon & coconut drizzle cake 212
lemon splits 140
minted courgette & lemon loaf 74
pear & ginger loaf with lemon glaze 160
pine nut, lemon & cardamom loaf 180
limes: sweet pineapple & lime loaf 160
linseeds: buckwheat, linseed & apricot bread 46
mixed seed bread 32
liquids 10
loaf sizes 14

madeira cake: cherry & almond 202
coffee & walnut 202
malt extract: date & malted barley bread 42
maple syrup: maple butter 166
mini pecan & maple loaves 30
marmalade cake 204
marzipan 184
cheat's stollen 214
hazelnut marzipan 150
nectarine & marzipan fruit küchen 184
stollen 150
meat: Italian wraps with mozzarella & cured meats 98
Mediterranean herb bread 62
mini dinner rolls 126
mini parsnip loaves 130

mini pecan & maple loaves 30
mini stollen bites 214
mint: feta, mint & cucumber rolls 124
minted courgette & lemon loaf 74
moist & fruity teacake 206
muesli bread 36
mushrooms: mushroom & mozzarella stromboli 50
pesto & mushroom tart 72
mustard: sweet dill & mustard loaf 52

naan breads: Peshwari naan 106
seeded naan breads 106
nectarine & marzipan fruit küchen 184

oatmeal: oatmeal & buttermilk bread 20
spicy apple parkin 210
oil 10
olive oil: olive oil, rosemary & raisin bread 62
semolina & olive oil bread 96
olives: olive & herb mini pittas 92
olive & tomato bread 70
Parmesan & olive bread sticks 104
pesto & marinated olive bread 88
pesto & olive dinner rolls 126
onions: feta & onion pide 102
goats' cheese & onion pizzas 80
onion & red Leicester bread 86
onion & tomato schiacciata 66

onion, sage & Gorgonzola focaccia 94
spicy chickpea & onion loaf 56
wholemeal carrot & onion loaves 130
orange: orange florentine loaf 180
poppy seed, orange & fig loaf 178
walnut & orange praline plait 174
orange liqueur, berry bread with 174

pancetta: pancetta & artichoke pizza 80
pancetta & Parmesan bread 70
pandolce 154
panettone 154
panzanella salad 44
paprika: chilli & smoked paprika bread 54
parkin: brandied prune parkin 210
spicy apple parkin 210
Parmesan & olive bread sticks 104
parsnips: mini parsnip loaves 130
party breads 144–57
pâté, creamy smoked salmon 52
peaches: spiced peach & redcurrant cake 188
peanut butter: spicy peanut & chilli loaf 54
pears: glazed pear & cinnamon loaf 224
pear & ginger loaf with lemon glaze 160
pear, cinnamon & raisin kügelhopf 186
pecan nuts: chocolate & pecan spiral 176
date & pecan teacake 206
mini pecan & maple loaves 30

pecan & apple rings 134
white chocolate & pecan cake 190
peppers: roasted red pepper cornbread 222
Peshwari naan 106
pesto: homemade sun-dried tomato pesto 66
pesto & marinated olive bread 88
pesto & mushroom tart 72
pesto & olive dinner rolls 126
pesto & pine nut bread 228
piadina 98
picnic slices: leek & Stilton 78
Provençal-style 78
pide, Turkish 102
pine nuts: pesto & pine nut bread 228
pine nut, lemon & cardamom loaf 180
pineapple: sweet pineapple & lime loaf 160
pissaladière 72
pistachio loaf with tropical fruits 182
pitta bread 92
olive & herb mini pittas 92
pizza: goats' cheese & onion 80
pancetta & artichoke 80
plaits: blueberry & vanilla 164
ciambella mandorlata 146
walnut & orange praline 146
plums: crumbly plum & ginger cake 194
spiced plum kügelhopf 186

pomegranate seeds: cranberry & pomegranate bread 46
poppy seeds: enriched poppy seed & lemon loaf 152
poppy seed, orange & fig loaf 178
potatoes: potato & thyme bread 82
spiced potato loaf 232
spicy potato bread 82
potted cheese 64
pretzels, salted 120
prosciutto & Parmesan crown 122
Provençal-style picnic slice 78
prunes: brandied prune & chocolate slice 176
brandied prune parkin 210
pumpkin: seeded pumpkin bread with Cajun spices 84

raisins: olive oil, rosemary & raisin bread 62
pear, cinnamon & raisin kügelhopf 186
raspberries: summer fruit cheesecake slice 188
red fruit & vanilla loaf 164
redcurrants: spiced peach & redcurrant cake 188
rich fruit teabread 168
ricotta cheese: blueberry & vanilla plait 164
ring loaf: Cheddar cheese & chutney ring 76
spinach & Manchego ring loaf 76
rolls: dark chocolate & ginger rolls 170
feta, mint & cucumber rolls 124

mini dinner rolls 126
pesto & olive dinner rolls 126
salt & pepper crusted rolls 138
sesame knots 128
spicy swirls 128
rosemary: garlic & rosemary twigs 120
olive oil, rosemary & raisin bread 62
rum butter, spiced 182
rye bread: fast-baked rye & caraway bread 38
toasted rye & smoked trout sandwich 38

sage: onion, sage & Gorgonzola focaccia 94
salad, panzanella 44
salt 10
grissini with aromatic salt 116
salt & pepper crusted rolls 138
salted pretzels 120
sandwich, toasted rye smoked trout 38
sauce, toffee 162
sausages: chorizo & broad bean tostadas 96
savarins, clementine & fig 136
savoury breads 48–89
schiacciata, onion & tomato 86
seeded cottage loaf 18
seeds: mixed seed bread 32
seeded banana loaf 178
seeded cheese batons 32
seeded gluten-free seeded naan breads 106
seeded pumpkin bread with Cajun spices 84
semolina & olive oil bread 96

sesame seeds: mixed seed bread 32
seeded gluten-free white bread 220
sesame knots 128
speedy sesame bread 24
simple gluten-free white bread 220
simple white loaf 18
slipper breads, spicy 56
smoked salmon pâté 52
smoked trout: toasted rye & smoked trout sandwich 38
sour cherry & almond rings 134
sourdough bread, easy 28
soured cream & berry bread 174
speedy sesame bread 24
speedy three grain bread 24
spice blend, baharat 110
spiced chickpea flatbreads 110
spiced fruit loaves 42
spiced peach & redcurrant cake 188
spiced plum kügelhopf 186
spiced potato loaf 232
spices 10–11
spicy apple parkin 210
spicy chicken mole with chilli bread 60
spicy chicken wraps 108
spicy peanut & chilli loaf 54
spicy potato bread 82
spicy slipper breads 56
spicy swirls 128
spinach: spinach & Manchego ring loaf 76
Stilton & spinach whirl 86
sticky Chelsea buns 172
sticky marmalade cake 204

sticky toffee & date loaf
162
Stilton & spinach whirl
86
stollen 150
cheat's stollen 214
mini stollen bites 214
strawberries: French
toast with yogurt,
strawberries & honey
20
stromboli: artichoke &
Gruyère 50
mushroom & mozzarella
50
sugar 10
beer & brown sugar
bread 64
sultanas: date, sultana &
hazelnut bread 196
sun-dried tomato & herb
bread 228
sun-dried tomato & herb
ciabatta 26
sunflower seeds: mixed
seed bread 32
seeded banana loaf
178
sunflower, yogurt &
apricot bread 226
sweet breads 158–99
sweet dill & mustard loaf
52
sweet pineapple & lime
loaf 160
sweet potato & tarragon
bread 84

tapenade & tomato
twist 58
tarragon: asparagus &
tarragon buns 132
sweet potato &
tarragon bread 84
tart, pesto & mushroom
72
teabread, rich fruit 168
teacakes: date & pecan
206
fruited 118
moist & fruity 206
three grain bread 24
thyme: potato & thyme
bread 82
toffee: homemade toffee
sauce 162
sticky toffee & date loaf
162
tomatoes: cherry tomato
& basil buns 132
homemade sun-dried
tomato pesto 66
olive & tomato bread
70
onion & tomato
schiacciata 66
sun-dried tomato &
herb bread 228
sun-dried tomato &
herb ciabatta 26
tapenade & tomato
twist 58
tomato focaccia 94
torte, crumbly blackberry
& apple 194

tostadas, chorizo & broad
bean 96
tropical fruits: breakfast
loaf with 226
pistachio loaf with 182
tropical fruit drizzle
cake 212
Turkish pide 102

vegetables: homemade
roasted vegetables
230
roasted vegetable loaf
with wild rice 230

walnuts: coffee & walnut
bread 166
coffee & walnut
madeira cake 202
walnut & honey bread
30
walnut & orange praline
plait 146
wheat bread, fast-baked
double 22
white bread: seeded
gluten-free white
bread 220
simple gluten-free
white bread 220
simple white loaf 18
white chocolate & banana
loaf 170
white chocolate & ginger
slice 224
white chocolate & pecan
cake 190

white chocolate cream
frosting 208
wholemeal carrot & onion
loaves 130
wholewheat flour 11
wild rice, roasted
vegetable loaf with
230
wraps: Italian wraps with
mozzarella & cured
meats 98
spicy chicken wraps
108
wreath, Greek Easter 148

yeast 9
yogurt: feta & yogurt dip
74
French toast with
yogurt, strawberries &
honey 20
sunflower, yogurt &
apricot bread 226
yogurt, honey & fennel
seed bread 44

acknowledgements

Executive Editor: Nicola Hill
Senior Editor: Lisa John
Executive Art Editor: Penny Stock
Designer: Cobalt
Photographer: William Shaw
Home Economist: Joanna Farrow
Props Stylist: Liz Hippisley
Production Controller: Carolin Stransky

Special photography: © Octopus Publishing
Group Limited/William Shaw.
Other photography: © Octopus Publishing Group
Limited/Ian Wallace 25, 47, 65, 87, 89, 141, 143,
175, 223, 227; /Stephen Conroy 23, 29, 45, 96, 101,
105, 117, 127, 153, 177, 185, 235.